WESTERN VISIONS, WESTERN FUTURES

WESTERN VISIONS, WESTERN FUTURES

PERSPECTIVES ON THE WEST IN CANADA

second edition

ROGER GIBBINS

and

LOLEEN BERDAHL

broadview press

National Library of Canada Cataloguing in Publication

Gibbins, Roger, 1947–
    Western visions, western futures : perspectives on the West in Canada / Roger Gibbins and Loleen Berdahl—2nd ed.

Originally published 1995 under title: Western visions.
Includes bibliographical references and index.
ISBN 1-55111-488-7

    1. Canada, Western—Politics and government. 2. Canada—Politics and government—1993.
I. Berdahl, Loleen, 1970– II. Title.

FC3219.G52 2003   971.2'03   C2003-902611-6
F1060.92.G53 2003

Broadview Press Ltd. is an independent, international publishing house, incorporated in 1985. Broadview believes in shared ownership, both with its employees and with the general public; since the year 2000 Broadview shares have traded publicly on the Toronto Venture Exchange under the symbol BDP.

We welcome comments and suggestions regarding any aspect of our publications–please feel free to contact us at the addresses below or at broadview@broadviewpress.com.

North America
PO Box 1243, Peterborough, Ontario, Canada K9J 7H5
Tel: (705) 743-8990; Fax: (705) 743-8353
email: customerservice@broadviewpress.com
3576 California Road, Orchard Park, NY, USA 14127

UK, Ireland, and continental Europe
Plymbridge Distributors Ltd.
Estover Road,
Plymouth, PL6 7PY, UK
Tel: (01752) 202301; Fax: (01752) 202333
email: orders@plymbridge.com

Australia and New Zealand
UNIREPS, University of New South Wales
Sydney, NSW, 2052
Tel: 61 2 9664 0999; Fax: 61 2 9664 5420
email: info.press@unsw.edu.au
www.broadviewpress.com

Broadview Press Ltd. gratefully acknowledges the financial support of the Government of Canada through the Book Publishing Industry Development Program for our publishing activities.

This book is printed on acid-free paper containing 30% post-consumer fibre.

Eco-Logo Certified
30 % Post.

PRINTED IN CANADA

CONTENTS

ACKNOWLEDGMENTS

In many ways, and not surprisingly, *Western Visions, Western Futures* reflects the personal experiences and odysseys of the authors. Roger Gibbins was raised in northern British Columbia, and completed his undergraduate degree at the University of British Columbia in Vancouver. Then, following graduate work at Stanford, he accepted a position in the Department of Political Science at the University of Calgary and is now President and CEO of the Canada West Foundation.

Loleen Berdahl arrived at the same destination through a very different route. She grew up in Saskatchewan and completed her undergraduate degree at the University of Saskatchewan in Saskatoon. Her interest in political science then drew her to the University of Calgary where she completed her PhD before signing on with the Canada West Foundation as Director of Research.

Our common location in the Canada West Foundation is not incidental to *Western Visions, Western Futures*. For over 30 years, Canada West, a non-partisan public policy research group based in Calgary, has grappled with the issues addressed in this book, and thus the work of the Foundation has infused our own thinking and perspectives. The book also draws heavily on CWF research and publications (see www.cwf.ca). For this reason, we must acknowledge the ongoing energy and reflections of our colleagues in the office, who have all contributed in many ways. Particular thanks goes to Robert Roach, who prepared the graphics for *Western Visions* and whose research work ripples through our analysis.

There are many other acknowledgments to be made. Sonia Arrison, now resident in San Francisco, was the co-author of *Western Visions*, published by Broadview Press in 1995 and the inspiration for the present work. The manuscript was reviewed by John Courtney, Faron Ellis, Herb Emery, Preston Manning, Phil Resnick, Robert Roach, and David Thomas, and was significantly improved through their comments. Betsy Struthers took the rough manuscript through the copy-editing process. Finally, thanks must be extended to our respective spouses, Isabel Gibbins and Troy Berdahl, for their enthusiasm for the project.

No matter how great the temptation, we cannot attribute any of the remaining weaknesses in the manuscript to those who have provided so much help along the way. Responsibility for errors and omissions remains with us.

The Canada West Foundation grants permission for the use of data figures from the publication *State of the West: Western Canadian Demographic and Economic Trends* (Robert Roach and Loleen Berdahl, Calgary, AB: Canada West Foundtion, 2001).

THE WEST IN CANADA
AND THE WORLD

"One might question why the West should be seen as a single unit. The main reasons, I think, are the size of the country, the history and the composition of its various communities, and the governmental system chosen by the fathers of Confederation. The national image of a single West has greater claim to existence today than at any time in Canadian history.... The West is an increasingly relevant regional generalization."[1]

— GERALD FRIESEN, historian

Introduction

The early twenty-first century does not reflect the optimistic globalization of the 1990s. In September 2001, the axis of international dialogue shifted from economics to security, and there are no indications that the shift is temporary. The efficient movement of goods has taken a backseat to monitoring the contents of trucks, trains, boats, and planes. The mobility of people — one of the hallmarks of globalization in the 1990s — has become more constrained, and additional security means that travel is less convenient than before. Immigration policies and the treatment of international refugees have become highly contested public policy issues. Predictions of a new economic order based on information technologies and a borderless world have met both market resistance and growing protectionism. Major powers, particularly the United States, have displayed an increased penchant for unilateralism in the international arena. And across the world deeply rooted historical conflicts thought to have been smothered by the relentless onslaught of globalization have flared anew.

There is no doubt that the international climate is evolving in an often turbulent fashion. The effects of globalization are not always benign, and, indeed, the notion of globalization itself is confronting ideological and political protest. In the face of this environment, it may be tempting to brush aside Canada's own internal challenges and to urge that Canadians focus on the larger global picture. Our own problems, it is often argued, pale beside those confronting other parts of the world. It would be a mistake, however, to draw a sharp line, or perhaps any line whatsoever, between world affairs and domestic politics. The essence of globalization is that global actions have local effects, sometimes dramatic in their impact, and that local actions have global ramifications. It would also be a mistake, therefore, to ignore either how global forces play out on the Canadian stage or how domestic politics affect our capacity to play on the international stage. Coming to grips with globalization engages domestic politics just as much as it engages the international domain.

The new global environment will test the evolving character of Canada on a variety of fronts. Managing the Canada-US trade relationship — one that has grown steadily in importance over the past ten years — is of great concern to all Canadian governments. Discussions of this relationship are in turn embedded within an overarching debate on continental integration, which concerns preserving not only national sovereignty but also the independence of Canadian monetary policy and some measure of autonomous policy space with respect to such matters as health care, immigration, environmental protection, and freedom of action on the world stage. Moreover, Canada continues to be tested by the "softer" aspects of globalization. For example, globalization has resulted, somewhat ironically, in the increased importance of cities,[2] thereby raising questions about the division of powers and responsibilities between not only two but potentially three orders of Canadian government. As the world comes into our living rooms through the communications revolution, concerns continue to be raised about protecting our national culture and identity — even as debates about defining both remain.

Our capacity to meet the challenges and opportunities incumbent in globalization will be determined in part by our ability to resolve internal challenges. These include public policy issues that tap into our national values, such as the sustainability of public health care and the Canada Pension Plan. They also include population aging, a shrinking tax base, continued socio-economic disparities among Aboriginal peoples, and labour supply shortages. And, almost inevitably it might seem, Canadian challenges continue to include regional disparities and discontent. None of these will evaporate magically under the bright lights of globalization. To the contrary, unless we are careful, they are likely to grow and impede our capacity to meet the challenges and seize the opportunities of a dynamic global environment. A house divided is unlikely to be a strong competitor in an increasingly competitive world economy.

Moreover, there is nothing in the logic of globalization to suggest the inevitable decline of regional communities, loyalties, or identities. In fact, globalization may enhance the saliency and appeal of communities more localized than existing nation states. In this context, Canada is perhaps more than ever a country of both provinces and regions. Although our geographic identities and affiliations are admittedly fluid, with regional identities coming into play most directly in relation to Canada as a whole or, more particularly, in relation to the federal government, the fluidity of regional identities does not diminish their relevance or importance. The country has a long history of territorially grounded discontent — Quebec separatism, western alienation, and, increasingly, Atlantic discontent. Despite its many successes in other fields, Canada has never dealt well with the root causes and policy manifestations of such discontent. Our track record when compared to that of other federal states of similar physical expanse, most notably Australia and the United States, is lamentable.[3] Poor performance in this respect limits our potential, saps our creative energies, and undermines national unity.

DEFINING WESTERN ALIENATION

Western alienation is a political ideology based on discontent with the West's subordinate position in the nation's cultural, economic, and political fabric, a position that frustrates regional aspirations and dreams. It embraces rather than rejects a sense of Canadian nationalism and expresses the desire, but not the institutional capacity, to play a larger role in national life. Western alienation reflects a search for recognition of the West's contribution to Canada in the past and its potential contribution to the country's future.

Regional strain has been felt most recently in the four western provinces of British Columbia, Alberta, Saskatchewan, and Manitoba. The early years of the new century have witnessed the sporadic eruption of separatist parties, an emaciated and frequently abrasive regional voice in the national Parliament, public arguments for provincial "firewalls," and seemingly endless radio programs, editorial commentary, and newspaper opinion pieces voicing regional discontent with the federal system and the federal government. Of course, this outpouring of regional and provincial discontent is not new; it reflects a long and convoluted history of grievance running back to the first years of European settlement. At the same time, and paradoxically to some observers, the West is thriving in many ways. The region has a relatively strong economy, is experiencing rapid urbanization, and has a generally high standard of living. Flows of interprovincial migration work to the region's benefit — between 1972 and 1999, for example, 488,252 more people voted with their feet to move into the West from other parts of Canada than left the West, and the intake of international immigration remains high, particularly in British Columbia. The West is not a region in despair. If anything, it is characterized by an abiding sense of optimism, a rich legacy of the region's frontier experience.

How, then, do we reconcile feelings of discontent and alienation with the facts of regional prosperity and optimism? This dichotomy has emerged as one of the most perplexing questions of modern Canadian politics. In short, what does the West want? *Western Visions, Western Futures* seeks to answer this question in two ways. First, we will unpack the baggage of western alienation to identify the key points of tension, with particular emphasis on those likely to continue in the years ahead. This unpacking will come through an examination of western Canadian politics, history, and public opinion and an assessment of the options available to address regional feelings of exclusion and disengagement. Second, we will highlight the opportunities and challenges present within the West itself, discussing how regional success in meeting these is vitally important to *all* Canadians. By addressing "What does the West want?," we encourage Canadians and their governments to begin a dialogue on lasting solutions to regional discontent *across* Canada.

The analysis will be directed to both the past and future. The historical part is not meant to provide a masochistic rehashing of old grievances. Rather, it illustrates the frequently close connection between past events and future trajectories. As Canadian historian Donald Creighton has written:

> The waves behind the vessel which is carrying humanity forward into the unknown ... can teach us where the winds of change are blowing and on what course the chief currents of our age are set. They can reveal to us the main direction of our voyage through time.[4]

In the case of the West, the currents set well in the past continue to shape the region's relationship with the broader national community. However, before we can predict where the western Canadian vessel might be heading, we need a better understanding of that vessel's basic structure, contents, and momentum.

The West in Canada

Given the immense array of public policy issues worthy of investigation, why focus on western Canada and its discontent? The simple answer is that the West accounts for a significant and growing proportion of Canada's population and economic activity. As Figure 1.1 shows, the West is the country's second most populous region, with a population at the time of the 2001 Census of just under nine million. It is smaller than Ontario but significantly larger than Quebec and almost four times the combined size of the Atlantic provinces. Admittedly, this population strength may be masked when we consider individual provinces. British Columbia, Canada's third largest province, accounted for only 13.0 per cent of the national population at the time of the 2001 Census; Alberta's share was 9.9 per cent, and Saskatchewan and Manitoba accounted for 3.3 per cent and 3.7 per cent respectively. However, the West as a region carries substantial demographic weight in the national community.

FIGURE 1.1   REGIONAL BREAKDOWN OF THE CANADIAN
POPULATION, 2001

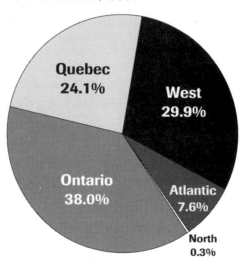

Source: Statistics Canada, Census 2001

Not incidentally, the fact that division into four separate provinces diminishes the region's demographic and therefore political strength was a key factor in the federal government's decision at the turn of the twentieth century to chop up the Northwest Territories into a number of discrete and smaller political units. The territorial premier, Frederick Haultain, supported the creation of a new province that would have included all of the land now occupied by Alberta, Saskatchewan, the Northwest Territories, and parts of Manitoba. (British Columbia, already a province, was not included in the Haultain plan.) Such a province would indeed have been a powerhouse within Confederation. Ottawa, however, pursued what can only be described as a divide-and-conquer strategy with the 1905 creation of both Alberta and Saskatchewan, the expansion of Manitoba, and the retention of the Northwest Territories under federal jurisdiction and control. A new province that might rival Ontario or Quebec was not in the offing.[5]

The West's demographic weight in Canada has been growing steadily, although not dramatically. As Figure 1.2 illustrates, the region's share of the national population has grown over the past three decades, while both Quebec and Atlantic Canada experienced significant declines. Thus, the country's population growth is tilted towards the West, although not to the exclusion of steady growth in Ontario. Western Canadians, particularly in Alberta and British Columbia, tend to exaggerate the degree of this tilt, perceiving a virtual cascade of people moving west rather than the reality of a steady, albeit modest, regional realignment of the national population.

Canada's regions differ not only in population size and growth rates but also in the composition of their populations. Quebec, for example, stands apart because of its linguistic character, whereas Toronto has made Ontario the primary destination for post-World War II immigration. The West's demographic base is distinctive in several important respects. The first feature of note is that almost two-thirds (62 per cent) of Canada's Aboriginal population resides in the West; indeed, according to the 2001 Census, more Aboriginal people live in Manitoba

FIGURE 1.2   CHANGES IN THE REGIONAL COMPOSITION OF
THE CANADIAN POPULATION, 1901-2000

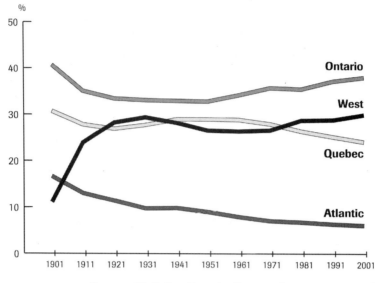

Source: Statistics Canada, Census data

(150,040) than live in the provinces of Quebec, Nova Scotia, New Brunswick, Newfoundland, and Prince Edward Island combined (133,530 Aboriginal persons). The Aboriginal population is significantly younger than the total population, and, while the non-Aboriginal population is aging steadily, the Aboriginal population recently experienced a "baby boom," with a relatively large proportion now under the age of 15. Given the Government of Canada's responsibility for "Indians and Lands reserved for Indians" (as specified in the Constitution Act), the high concentration of Aboriginal people in western Canada makes the region of particular federal importance.

A second feature to note is that western Canada provides the demographic foundation for national multiculturalism. Unlike eastern and central Canada, regions settled predominantly from the "motherlands" of England and France, western Canada has a long and strong history of multiculturalism, which did not end with the massive influx of primarily European immigrants around the turn of the last century but continues through to current patterns of non-European immigration. Although this runs contrary to popular conceptions of western Canada as a "redneck monolith," there is no denying the data. According to the 2001 Census, western Canada is home to four of Canada's five large cities (census metropolitan areas) with the highest proportion of visible minorities (the top five are, in order, Vancouver, Toronto, Abbotsford, Calgary, and Edmonton), and, as Figure 1.3 illustrates, 14 per cent of the West's total population identifies itself with a visible minority, compared to 13 per cent for the rest of Canada.[6] That said, it must be acknowledged that the four western provinces vary greatly in the proportion of the population identifying as a visible minority, from a high of 22 per cent in British Columbia to a low of 3 per cent in Saskatchewan. (These differences reflect the West's immigration patterns.)

FIGURE 1.3   ETHNIC DIVERSITY, WEST, AND THE REST OF CANADA

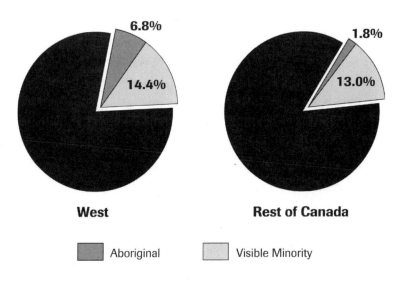

Source: Statistics Canada, Census 1996

One area in which the West does *not* stand apart from other regions is in the urban-rural mix of its population. Despite common perceptions to the contrary, the West's population is not notably rural. In fact, at the time of the 2001 Census, the West had a level of urbanization on par with the national average and within a few decimal points of the Ontario experience. Large metropolitan centres dominate the demographic landscape in the West, as they do elsewhere in Canada. While the rural West retains a great deal of importance and faces a troubling set of public policy challenges, it no longer characterizes the region as a whole.

If the region's demographic weight and diversity are insufficient reasons to pay attention to western Canada, one might also consider the importance of its economy. The West is endowed with a resource base that is the envy of most nations. There are substantial high-grade deposits of minerals including lead, copper, zinc, potash, uranium, molybdenum, gold, and silver. The region is not only Canada's primary source of petroleum, natural gas, and coal, but it also has huge hydro-electric potential. The rich prairie soil is the nation's major producer of grains — wheat, barley, oats — in addition to forage and pulse crops, oil seeds, potatoes, and sugar beets. The more arid parts support substantial herds of cattle and feed lot operations for both cattle and hogs. The northern temperate rainforests of coastal British Columbia, together with the inland forests, provide the bulk of Canada's production of softwood lumber and pulp and paper.

Given this natural resource base, it is not surprising that western Canada's contribution to the national economy is proportionate to its share of the national population. In per capita GDP terms, the West's growth over the past 30 years has exceeded that of the rest of Canada, with a great deal of the West's economic growth occurring in the 1990s (see Figure 1.4). Like other regions, the West is increasingly active as an exporter. As Chapter 4 will discuss in more detail, all four western provinces have seen their international export activities increase since 1981, in both proportionate and absolute terms. Overall, in 1999, western Canada generated $84.3 billion in international exports and $52.4 billion in interprovincial exports — representing an important national economic interest.

FIGURE 1.4   PER CAPITA GDP GROWTH, 1971 AND 1999
(with % change)

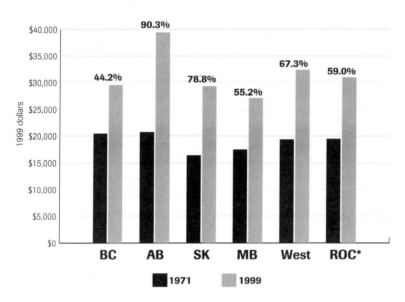

Source: Roach and Berdahl

It is clear that the four western provinces together carry substantial demographic and economic weight in the national community. This conclusion, however, begs an essential question: is it more appropriate to treat western Canada as a coherent region or simply as four geographically congruent provinces? Is the West truly a region? Or, given the very real provincial differences that continue to exist, under what conditions and circumstances does it make sense to think of the four western provinces as a single regional community?

The West as a Region

The West, like many regional and most national communities, takes on greater cohesion and homogeneity the farther one moves away. The closer you get to the land and its people, the more the region begins to fragment first into quite distinctive provincial communities and then into a multitude of communities within the provinces themselves. No one, for example, would confuse Regina with Vancouver or, within British Columbia, Prince George with Victoria. Thus to view the West up close is like looking into a kaleidoscope where the brightly coloured pieces overwhelm the regional pattern. And yet, despite often-competing interests and sharply etched community differences, the West maintains a degree of coherence and some reasonable measure of distinctiveness from other regional communities in Canada. Both the regional glue and distinctiveness, we suggest, come less from the region's varied geography and more from how western Canadians see the world, particularly the political world. In David Smith's evocative prose, the *prairie* West is best seen as "a region of the mind":

> ... it is at the level of public consciousness that the region has achieved its lasting identity. Visually, to anyone traveling between the rim of the Shield and the foothills of the Rockies across a thousand miles of "black soil sliding into open sky," the Prairies merge as one vast land. For those who have never seen the Canadian plains but know their history and literature, the region is myth, of the mind.... 7

To a significant degree, we argue, this description applies to the western Canadian region as a whole, inclusive of British Columbia. There is a region of the mind that under some, although by no means all, conditions transcends the particular circumstances of provincial communities.

It is this region of the mind that allows the West — four provinces, each with varying economic fortunes, unique histories, and dynamic political cultures, contained in a vast geography with two very distinct landscapes and climates (prairies and mountains) — to manifest itself as a region. Diversity has not meant that a regional identity has failed to take root. Indeed, in all fairness, one might argue that the West is no more diverse a region than is Ontario — the chief difference between the two being that the West elects four provincial governments to Ontario's one.

Regional Identities

Public opinion research shows that western Canadians see the West very much in a regional light and that this perception has held over time. In a 1977 public opinion study, roughly four in five western Canadians across all four provinces felt that there was a "very or moderately strong ... sense of regional identity" in the West.[8] The proportion ranged from 77 per cent in Manitoba to 90 per cent in Alberta. (Interestingly, this national study found respondents in all provinces reporting strong regional identities, with Atlantic Canada at 78 per cent, Quebec at 86 per cent, and Ontario at 76 per cent.) In a 2001 Canada West Foundation survey of over 3,200 western Canadians, conducted almost a quarter of a century later and under very different political and economic circumstances, similar perceptions were found.[9] As Figure 1.5 shows, most western Canadians agree with the statement, "The West is a distinct region, different in many ways from the rest of Canada." Variability in opinion across the four western provinces is strikingly modest. What is not modest is the clear emergence of a regional frame for citizen identities.

FIGURE 1.5   REGIONAL IDENTITIES IN THE WEST, 2001

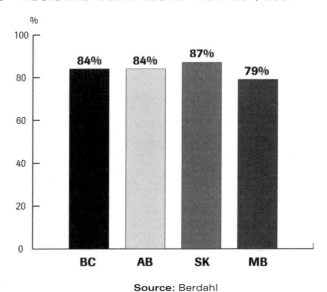

Source: Berdahl

This is not to say that regional identities take precedence over local, provincial, or national identities. Seeing the West as a distinct region and identifying oneself *primarily* as a western Canadian are two different things. As in other regions of the country, a significantly larger proportion of survey respondents identify themselves as Canadians before identifying themselves regionally. However, it is possible that a growing number of western Canadians are beginning to identify first with the region. Although the 1977 and 2001 surveys noted above are not directly comparable due to different question wordings and response options, it is interesting that in 1977 approximately 8 per cent of western Canadian respondents identified with the region first, ahead of Canada or their province. (The provincial proportions were 6 per cent in British Columbia, 7 per cent in Alberta, 15 per cent in Saskatchewan, and 9 per cent in Manitoba.) In the 2001 Canada West survey (Figure 1.6), 12 per cent of western Canadian respondents identify themselves primarily as western Canadians ahead of local, provincial, national, continental, or international

FIGURE 1.6   PRIMARY IDENTIFICATIONS WITHIN THE WEST, 2001, (percentage selecting "western Canada")

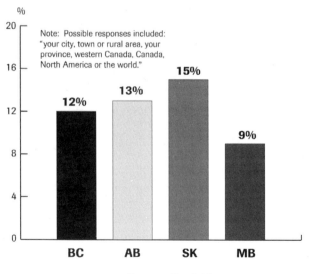

Note: Possible responses included: "your city, town or rural area, your province, western Canada, Canada, North America or the world."

Source: Berdahl

identities. Given the larger range of response options in the 2001 survey, it is reasonable to assume that regional identifications have become more common over time.[10]

Regional Patterns

As much as the West is a region of the mind, it must be stressed that it is not *only* a region of the mind. There are a number of social, demographic, and economic patterns that both tie the four western provinces together and set them apart from other provinces in Canada.

First, western Canadians tend to have a strong history of familial and social ties with other provinces in the region. Many have family residing in another western province or grew up in a different western Canadian province before moving to their current location. As Figures 1.7 and 1.8 illustrate, the majority of western Canadians who decide to move to another province actually move within the West, while the majority of Canadians moving into a western province also come from within the region. This *regional* population churn reinforces regional loyalties and identities. As western Canadians move within the region, they tend to retain a level of affection and concern for their "home province" and will often travel among the four provinces to visit family and friends. Indeed, this high level of intra-regional mobility leads many Calgary commentators to quip that at Calgary-Saskatchewan or Calgary-Winnipeg football games, it is difficult to ascertain who the home team truly is.

Second, western Canadians not only travel and move frequently within the region; they also trade. As noted earlier, the region continues to have a high level of interprovincial trade — $52.4 billion in 1999, or roughly 20 per cent of the region's GDP. Approximately one-half of that interprovincial trade was among the four western provinces themselves, making for a vibrant intra-regional economy.

Third, there are a number of demographic patterns common to the region, including a recent wave of urbanization. While the West is

FIGURE 1.7   DESTINATION OF INTERPROVINCIAL MIGRANTS,
1972–1999

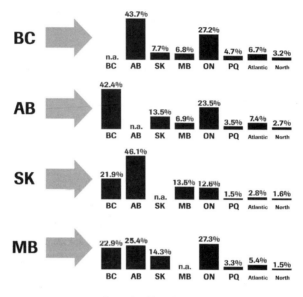

Source: Roach and Berdahl

FIGURE 1.8   ORIGIN OF INTERPROVINCIAL MIGRANTS,
1972–1999

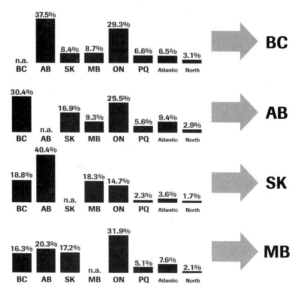

Source: Roach and Berdahl

currently as urbanized as the rest of Canada, such urbanization is a relatively new regional phenomenon, with the number of people moving to urban areas growing rapidly over the past 30 years. By contrast, Ontario and Quebec experienced much more gradual urbanization. What this means in a practical sense is that the western provinces and cities must deal with a number of policy issues resulting from rapid urban growth — highly stressed urban infrastructures, changing demography, and the need to balance urban and rural needs. However, one of the challenges facing the West — both within and outside the region — is the general lack of recognition of its urban face. This is a theme to which we will return in the chapters to come.

FIGURE 1.9   PERCENTAGE OF THE REGIONAL POPULATION LIVING IN URBAN AREAS, 1966 AND 2001

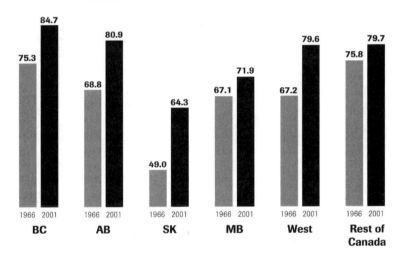

Source: Statistics Canada, Census data

Another example of the unique demographic reality of western Canada, as mentioned above, is the relatively high concentration of Aboriginal people. This concentration benefits the western provinces in several ways; not only is the regional culture enriched, but, because the Aboriginal population is significantly younger than the general population, there is a large labour pool of Aboriginal youth available. However, it also means that Aboriginal public policy issues such as land claims, the implementation of self-government, socio-economic dispar- ity, and the growing number of urban Aboriginal people are of greater importance and urgency in the West than in other regions. Western Canada also must deal more directly with racism and with the often tense relationship between the Aboriginal and non-Aboriginal commu- nities, a relationship that western Canadians are more likely to charac- terize as deteriorating than as improving (Figure 1.10).

FIGURE 1.10   PERCEPTIONS OF THE ABORIGINAL/NON- ABORIGINAL RELATIONSHIP

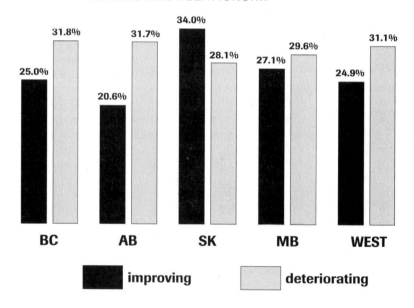

Survey Question: Do you think relations between Aboriginal peoples and other Canadians are improving, deteriorating, or staying about the same?

Source: Berdahl

A fourth regional commonality is the relatively heavy reliance on the "old," resource-based economy. Unlike the central Canadian economy, western Canadian trade is predominantly based on natural resources — a somewhat difficult position given that commodity prices in the resource sector are notoriously unstable. Figure 1.11 shows the Statistics Canada price indices for raw materials and industrial products. While the coverage of the raw materials index does not coincide perfectly with the resource mix in western Canada, it is sufficiently close to illustrate the greater volatility of resource commodity prices. Price instability in the resource sector translates into substantial swings in profits, taxes, investment, and employment. Uncertainty is therefore endemic to the regional economy — a reality less prevalent in the central Canadian economy with its broader industrial base. Resource trade also exposes a common reliance on a complex regional transportation system connecting western Canadian producers to distant continental and global markets.

FIGURE 1.11 VARIABILITY IN COMMODITY PRICES FOR RAW MATERIALS AND INDUSTRIAL PRODUCTS January 1981–March 2001 (1992=100)

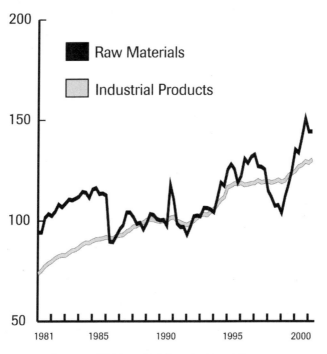

Source: Gibbins, *Building the New West*

A final commonality worth noting here is the regional aspiration for *equality* within Confederation. This quest goes back to the quasi-colonial terms of western settlement and to the hard-fought battle to secure provincial ownership of natural resources on terms identical to the founding provinces. Equality is a theme in western Canadian life that reaches far beyond the promotion of equal provincial representation in the Senate; it is one that taps a deeply embedded belief that the West is not treated equally when it comes to the financial decisions and programs of the federal government. While the conditions of the four western provinces may differ markedly, they are bridged by a common perception that unequal regional treatment by Ottawa is a shared reality and grievance.

"We are a small region of less than ten million people. We cannot afford to split the West into more than one economy."
— Hon. Allan Blakeney, former Premier of Saskatchewan[11]

These are but a few examples of the patterns that tie the West together as a region and stand it apart from the rest of Canada. Many others, including nascent institutional structures, will be discussed in the chapters that follow. Our point is not that region trumps province in the West, for there are many instances in which provincial interests, political cultures, identities, and organizational patterns prevail. In a similar fashion, there are many instances in which national interests, political cultures, identities, and organizational patterns prevail. The more subtle point is that in many, though by no means all, circumstances there is also a regional reality that competes for cultural, economic, identity, and political space. It is to this regional reality that *Western Visions, Western Futures* is directed.

Western Visions: Framing the Discussion

It is not surprising that a highly diverse country with a small population spread across a large landmass will experience different regional realities, expectations, and aspirations. Nor is it surprising that territorially based discontent will emerge from this stew. Probably the best evidence for this comes from Quebec, where a territorial frame gave linguistic conflict a very different dynamic than would have been the case in a unitary state. For decades, many Quebecers felt their interests and aspirations were not adequately reflected in the Canadian community or by the federal government. Quebec was not seen by its residents as a province like the others, but winning recognition of this perception within the constitutional and institutional fabric of the Canadian federal state has proven to be an extremely difficult task. The resultant discontent and resentment led to the Quiet Revolution in the 1960s, followed by a generation of intense nationalist politics from which the country has yet to fully recover.

Western alienation is another example of regional discontent. The next chapter examines the economic, social, and political roots of the discontent that has built up in the West since the early days of settlement. As we will show, a number of common themes have woven their way through the region's history — themes expressed by an array of political movements and actors. There has often been an explosive mix of fact and fiction: political perceptions have not been simple reflections of the realities of the day (whatever they may be), but rather reflections of those realities as seen by an often biased, even jaundiced, regional population. While we will certainly argue that there is substance to regional discontent with the place of the West in the broader national fabric, it is not our intention to provide a detailed empirical investigation of the realities of Confederation. Rather, we want to explore how western Canadians *see* the world; the accuracy of those perceptions is a matter of secondary interest.

Chapter 3 provides an empirical face to the pillars of western alienation identified in Chapter 2. It traces western Canadian public opinion
over the past three decades to show that while policy debates, political
realities, and economic strengths have shifted considerably over time,
feelings of western alienation have not subsided. Chapter 4 then moves
on to consider strategic options and alternatives for dealing with western alienation. Here the emphasis is placed on the national government,
the national party system, and provincial governments in the West.

Chapter 5 shifts gears somewhat to address the western Canadian
policy agenda. More specifically, it examines both the policy priorities
of the region and the potential policy flash-points that may fuel alienation or provide opportunities for cooperation. Chapter 6 pursues this
latter theme in greater detail by exploring the opportunities and potential for regional governance in an increasingly interdependent world.
The concluding chapter comments briefly on the West and the future
of Canada. What can we expect if the status quo prevails? As *Western
Visions* will demonstrate, the ties that bind the West to Canada are
becoming frayed. It is difficult, therefore, to look ahead with unbridled
optimism unless national political leaders begin to bring a greater sense
of regional equity and fairness to national political life.

It must be stressed that we have no pretensions about writing a comprehensive history of western Canada or even of painting a detailed picture
of the region's political landscape. There is no dearth of excellent historical works on the Canadian West and no shortage of astute political
commentary. Our objectives are more limited: to describe the evolution
and contemporary nature of regional discontent and aspirations in western Canada and to discuss ways to harness both to the benefit of the West
and the country as a whole. We also hope to place the West within the
Canadian context, and do so in a fashion that will be accessible to those
who live within the region and to others who wish to strengthen their
understanding of its political life. Indeed, the larger audience may be
particularly important, for the "western visions" discussed in the chapters
to come have a relevance that reaches well beyond the region itself.

Notes

1   Gerald Friesen, *The West: Regional Ambitions, National Debates, Global Age* (Toronto, ON: Penguin, 1999) 185.

2   Katherine Harmsworth, *Glocalism: The Growing Importance of Local Space in the Global Environment* (Calgary, AB: Canada West Foundation, December 2001).

3   The United States, admittedly, fought a civil war prior to Canada's creation. Thus, any assumption of greater American success in handling territorially based discontent is limited to the post-1867 period.

4   Donald Creighton, *The Passionate Observer: Selected Writings* (Toronto, ON: McClelland and Stewart, 1980) 19.

5   The federal government's "divide and conquer" strategy may have begun even earlier when Ottawa carved the Yukon Territory out of the Northwest Territory at the time of the Klondike gold rush.

6   Statistics Canada does not classify Aboriginal peoples as visible minorities. Therefore, the data presented do not include Aboriginal persons.

7   David E. Smith, "The Prairie Provinces," *The Provincial Political Systems: Comparative Essays*, ed. David J. Bellamy, Jon H. Pammett, and Donald C. Rowat (Toronto, ON: Methuen, 1976) 46. This phrase was also used by Richard Allen, ed., *A Region of the Mind* (Regina, SK: Canadian Plains Study Centre, 1973).

8   Martin Goldfarb, *The Searching Nation: A Study of Canadians' Attitudes to the Future of Confederation* (Toronto, ON: Southam Press, 1977).

9   For a detailed description of this survey and its methodology, see Loleen Berdahl, *Looking West: A Survey of Western Canadians* (Calgary, AB: Canada West Foundation, 2001).

10 Public opinion surveys tend to limit response categories to "provincial" or "national" or, in rare cases, "regional," and the result is typically an inflated number of respondents selecting a national identity. The inclusion of a "local" option significantly deflates the national proportion.

11 Roger Gibbins, *Building the New West: A Framework for Regional Prosperity* (Calgary, AB: Canada West Foundation, 2001).

CHAPTER 2

THE ROOTS OF
WESTERN ALIENATION

"I think western Canada very much wants to be part of the
national debate. Western Canada is growing, it's strong, it's vigorous, it has solutions and ideas to bring to the table. And it wants
to do that. I think its frustration is that the central government,
the West believes, is utterly indifferent to the ideas and the aspirations that western Canada wants to put on the table in the
national debate."[1]

—DIANE ABLONCZY,
Canadian Alliance MP for Calgary Nose Hill.

Introduction

Although the early settlement and current prosperity of western Canada
have been remarkable success stories, they have also been accompanied
by pervasive discontent over the region's place within the broader national
community. Western Canadians have argued with a great deal of passion
that their political influence fails to reflect the West's economic and
demographic weight. Alienation, however, has not sparked any widespread desire to withdraw from Canada through either lower rates of
participation in national politics or support for separatist movements. To

the contrary, it drives a determined effort to reposition the region *within* the cultural, economic, and political fabric of Canadian life. The goal is national treatment that is fair and equitable. Simply put, "the West wants in" from the political cold, but in on its own terms.[2]

Regional discontent is not an abstract concern but rather one that relates directly to the strategic positioning of the region within the new global (and continental) economy. Of necessity, this positioning takes place in part through the national economy and political system. Many of the West's linkages to the global economy are shaped by policies of the federal government; thus, how the West is treated nationally bears directly on its competitive position globally. This was particularly so in the past when the federal government set tariffs, provided the policy framework and much of the funding for a national transportation system, and established the immigration policies that settled the West. While the regional impact of federal policy has weakened in an era of progressive globalization — trade policy, for example, is now largely set within the context of the North American Free Trade Agreement (NAFTA) and the World Trade Organization (WTO) if not unilaterally by the United States — national policies still have significant, albeit diminished, impact on the global positioning of western Canada. As a consequence, debates about the place of the West within the broader Canadian community are much more than a rehashing of past grievances; they are debates about future aspirations, about challenges and policy capacity in fluid continental and global environments, about the prospects for regional prosperity. Therefore, understanding regional discontent is as much about unlocking the future as it is about unlocking the past.

Nor are debates about the place of the West irrelevant for Canadians living outside western Canada. Given the region's share of the national population and its contribution to the national economy, debates about *regional prosperity* are really debates about *national prosperity*. (The West's population at the time of the 2001 Census equaled the combined populations of Quebec, New Brunswick, Nova Scotia, and Prince Edward Island.) Canadians at large have a real and immediate stake in the West and in coming to grips with the complex dynamics of regional discontent. After all, many may move west, and many have relatives and friends in western Canada.

How, then, can we get a conceptual handle on *western alienation*? How can we unpack the phrase? One approach would be to catalogue past grievances and contemporary public policy disputes, assuming that the resultant litany would be self-explanatory. Where there is so much policy smoke, there must also be the smouldering coals of western alienation. This approach has considerable appeal. Outrage with the 1980 imposition of the National Energy Program is one classic example, but only one of scores of national policies over the years that western Canadians took to be hostile to regional interests and aspirations. However, the sheer number of such disputes and their persistence over time illustrate the difficulty in trying to account for western alienation by policy-specific explanations. Individual policy grievances are drops in a much larger bucket and are best seen as symptoms of deeper institutional and political distress. Certainly this is how they are perceived within the West. It is the pattern behind the specific grievances that is important.

WESTERN ALIENATION AS A LEARNED RESPONSE

"I came to the West in the 1980s. I moved from Montreal. So I saw Quebec separation there and chose Alberta as my home. I had heard about western alienation when I was in law school in Quebec, and didn't understand what it could possibly be about given the more acute form of alienation that I had studied when I was in eastern Canada. And I must say that when I came here and had my first federal election, and turned on the television and at 8:01, when not a single vote in Alberta had been counted, and I was told there was a majority government, I got it, for the first time. My vote wasn't counted and already I knew what was going to happen to the country."[3]

— Sheilah Martin, Professor of Law at the University of Calgary

The essence of western alienation is to be found less in the accumulation of policy grievances than in the political system that creates such grievances in the first place. In the words of Vancouver columnist Ilana Mercer, "The discontent Westerners experience lies not in the substance of the issues, but in the process itself."[4] Although the steady accretion of specific grievances counts, it is the cumulative story they tell that is more important. This does not mean that contemporary regional discontent is incapable of being moderated or indeed exacerbated through public policies. To the contrary, and as Chapter 5 discusses in detail, the contemporary policy agenda is ripe with both opportunities and challenges in both respects. Still, the symptomatic character of specific policy disputes must be stressed. The failure to grant provincial ownership of natural resources until 1930, the NEP, freight rates, the National Policy (discussed below), and, most recently, at least in Alberta, the Kyoto Accord all represent more than policy grievances; they are potent symbols, interpretative milestones in the West's rocky relationship with the federal government and the larger Canadian community. This helps explain why positive progress by the federal government on individual policy files often yields little return in terms of the overall tone and level of regional discontent. As the old saying goes, it takes more than one swallow to make a spring.

Over time, a comprehensive regional critique emerged in the West that tied specific policy grievances to the nature of Canadian party politics, federalism, and parliamentary institutions. This critique first developed in step with the agricultural settlement of the prairie provinces when a core set of economic grievances, laced with cultural conflict, characterized the early decades of the grain economy. These grievances led in turn to the charge that national policies exacerbated rather than moderated a host of challenges confronting the pioneer community. The critique sank deeply into the regional political culture because so many western Canadians were linked directly or indirectly to the grain economy that dominated the region. And, because the grievances were so widely shared, the critique was easily communicated. It then took on new dimensions as Canada moved through a period of dramatic social change and constitutional upheaval in the latter half of the twentieth century. Rather than being discarded as a relic of the early years of the grain economy, the regional critique took on renewed vigor for western Canadians still lacking an effective voice in the national political system.

WHAT DOES THE WEST WANT?

Peter Menzies, Editor-in-Chief of the Calgary Herald, provides an Alberta-centric answer to this question with four simple statements:[5]
- A prime minister who actually cares.
- Give us our money back.
- Stop making fun of us because we believe in hard work and self-reliance and prefer personal liberty to collectivism.
- Leave us alone.

It is not altogether clear whether western Canadians outside Alberta would agree with all four of his points, although they would certainly agree with the first.

Thus, western alienation has deep historical roots; it has been shaped by, and has been used to explain, a multitude of conflicts between the settler communities in the West and their national government. A common thread runs through this long evolution: the rules of the political game are tipped against the best interests of the nearly one in three Canadians who live to the west of the Great Lakes. This was (and is) particularly irksome to western Canadians who believe, not always accurately, that in other respects the country is tipped with people, economic opportunities, wealth, and political creativity flowing across the country to the West, indeed, across the Prairies to the Pacific coast. All that defies this natural gravitational force is political power, which remains firmly lodged in Ontario and Quebec. Optimism and frustration, therefore, are two faces of the same coin; western alienation makes sense only when placed against the backdrop of a regional community proud of its past and optimistic about its future.

The most salient backdrop for an understanding of the historic roots of western alienation comes from the agrarian community on the Prairies during the first three decades of the twentieth century. As Figure 2.1 illustrates, the great bulk of the western Canadian population at that time lived on the prairies; British Columbia's demographic dominance is a more recent phenomenon. It is, then, to the prairie community that we now turn to find the initial roots of western alienation.

FIGURE 2.1: PROVINCIAL DISTRIBUTION OF THE WESTERN CANADIAN POPULATION, 1931 AND 2001

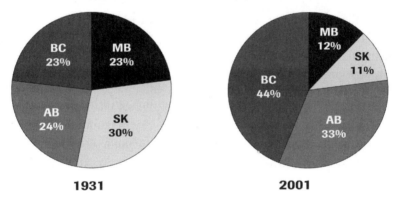

In the early part of the twentieth century, the West's demographic centre of gravity was on the Prairies. At the time of the 1931 Census, for example, only 2 of 10 western Canadians lived in British Columbia, compared to 3 in Saskatchewan and 2.5 in both Alberta and Manitoba. Today, close to one in two western Canadians live in British Columbia. As a consequence, the degree to which British Columbians are part of the broader regional community — the degree to which they see themselves as western Canadians — is a critically important matter.

Source: Statistics Canada, Census data

Agrarian Roots of Regional Discontent

Arthur Lower's history of Canada, *From Colony to Nation*,[6] traces the country's slow and peaceful evolution from British colony to an independent country spanning the top end of North America. Within this

national story is embedded the story of the West's slower emergence as
an equal partner in Canada,[7] and this latter story also bears the imprint
of colonization, albeit internal colonization. Admittedly, the language
of colonization must be used with a great deal of care. The typical
outcome of de-colonization is the creation of an independent state, and
this has never been a goal for more than a small handful of western
Canadians. Both British Columbia and Manitoba, moreover, were early
members of Confederation, and the "colonized" in western Canada
were those who immigrated to the region from abroad or migrated
there from other parts of Canada.[8] Nonetheless, the notion of colonization alerts us to some important themes in the early history of the
West. The region was in many ways the creation of the federal government and its policies, it was a debtor region with debt largely held by
central Canadian financial institutions, and western Canadians
confronted a national government that was geographically and psychologically distant from their own region and concerns. The provincial
ownership of natural resources, a constitutional entitlement bestowed
on the founding provinces at the time of Confederation, was not realized for the prairie provinces until the 1930 *Natural Resources Transfer
Act*. Although the history of the West was not the colonization experienced by many parts of the developing world, in broad outline it often
seemed to walk and quack like the duck of colonization.

The colonialization theme is nicely illustrated in an editorial that
appeared in the Toronto *Globe* on March 6, 1862:

> When the territory [the West] belongs to Canada, when its navi-
> gable waters are traversed for a few years by vessels, and lines of
> travel are permanently established, when settlements are formed
> in favourable locations throughout the territory, it will not be diffi-
> cult by grants of land to secure the construction of a railway across
> the plains and through the mountains. . . . If we set about the work
> of opening the territory at once, we will win the race [against the
> United States] . . . It is an empire we have in view, and its whole

export and import trade will be concentrated in the hands of Canadian merchants and manufacturers if we strike for it now.[9]

Attitudes in Ontario may have changed over the past 140 years, of course! Nonetheless, strains of the colonialization theme still ripple through, leading Don Smiley, one of Canada's foremost political scientists, to conclude that "Western Canada was from the first, and to a considerable extent remains, an economic colony of the country's central heartland."[10]

THE AMERICAN CONTRAST

In many respects, the American West paralleled the Canadian experience: it too was a creation of the federal government and its policies, a debtor region that was psychologically distant from the national government. Furthermore, and unlike the Canadian case, most of the public lands in the western mountain states still fall under the control of the federal government's Bureau of Land Management. However, these features have not generated the prolonged and pervasive sense of alienation that we find in western Canada. Why is this the case? A variety of explanations come to mind. First, small states in the American West have enjoyed effective representation in the US Senate, a situation that has no parallel in Canada where the appointed Senate is, at best, inconsequential. Second, there has been no American parallel to the dominance of Ontario in Canadian politics, no single state that contains close to 40 per cent of the national population, constitutes the economic heartland, dominates the national media, and provides the site of the national capital. The largest American state, California, contains only 10 per cent of the American population, and it is a western state. Third, there has been no American parallel to Quebec's dominance of the national political agenda, no single state or indeed single region against which the western states might unite in opposition. Fourth, the American West has been woven into the very tapestry and symbolism of the American experience. In many respects, the United States is the American West writ large; the western experience has shaped and defined American values. The western experience in Canada has not had a similar impact on national values or mythologies.

Given this dependent relationship, the central question confronting western Canadians was whether national policies were a help or hindrance as they faced the challenges of an often hostile agrarian frontier. Simply put, was Ottawa friend or foe? To answer this question we need a rudimentary understanding of both the population that settled western Canada and the regional economy it created. Our focus here is on the prairie provinces which, until after World War II, contained the great bulk of the regional population and provided the heartland for the regional economy. The foundations for western alienation were laid on the Prairies.

The Population Base of the Prairie West

At the time of the 1901 Census, less than 8 per cent of the Canadian population lived on the Prairies, and over 60 per cent of those lived in Manitoba. Population growth following Confederation had been slow in the West; although the prairies were linked to the rest of Canada by the Canadian Pacific Railroad, international immigration had been sluggish because of the availability of open land in the United States and a global economic depression. However, by the turn of the century open land in the United States had largely disappeared, the global depression was lifting, and experience had shown that the intemperate prairie climate could indeed support agriculture. In response, international immigrants began to arrive by the hundreds of thousands. From 1901 to 1913, 2,500,000 immigrants poured into Canada, compared to only 1,500,000 over the previous 33 years,[11] and the majority headed west. In the single decade from 1901 to 1911, the prairie population grew by an astounding 316 per cent. By 1931 the population of Saskatchewan had grown to almost a million people, a tenfold increase from 1901 that made Saskatchewan Canada's third largest province. It is no wonder that this explosive population growth was accompanied by an unbounded sense of optimism in the "last, best west."[12]

Not surprisingly, the prairie population was largely rural. Although the rural share of the population fell from 75.4 per cent in 1901 to 61.9

per cent in 1941, the latter figure compared to a 1941 rural population in Ontario of only 38.3 per cent. More notable was the ethnic complexity of the prairie population compared to that of Ontario. Table 2.1 contrasts the ethic composition of the prairie and Ontario populations at the time of the 1931 Census, which marked the effective ethnic crystalization of the Prairies for the next 40 years. As can be seen, the prairie population was much more diverse than was Ontario's. Not only was the British component much smaller, but so too was the French component. (Migration from Ontario had bolstered the British population in the West, but there was no comparable migration from Quebec.) As a consequence, those of French descent on the Prairies became one of many ethnic groups, and by no means the largest, making up the regional population. The English and French dominance of the central Canadian population was not replicated on the Prairies where blocks of land were reserved for immigrants from England, Scotland, Germany, Russia, the Ukraine, Belgium, Scandinavia, and Iceland. True, those of British descent numerically dominated both Ontario and the West, but dominance was less pronounced in the latter case.

The immigrants not listed in Table 2.1 are Americans. Census records at the time did not record "American" as an ethnic origin; therefore, immigrants from the United States were classified ethnically by the last country in which their ancestors lived before immigrating to the United States. (Someone whose ancestors had arrived from the Netherlands in the 1700s and who then had immigrated to the Canadian Prairies in 1911 would show up in the Canadian census as Dutch, not American.) Nonetheless, the number of American immigrants settling on the Prairies, some of whom were repatriated Canadians from Ontario and Quebec, was substantial. At the time of the 1931 Census, it was estimated that there were 18,000 Americans in Manitoba, 73,000 in Saskatchewan, and 79,000 in Alberta. American immigrants were the source of many of the radical ideas that fed populist thought in the Canadian West.

The prairie population was not only more diverse than the population of Ontario, but was also more likely to be foreign-born, something

TABLE 2.1:   ETHNIC COMPOSITION OF THE PRAIRIE AND
              ONTARIO POPULATIONS, 1931 [13]

	PRAIRIES	ONTARIO
British Isles	50.8%	74.0%
French	5.8	8.7
German	10.3	5.1
Scandinavian	6.9	0.6
Ukrainian	8.2	0.7
Hebrew	1.2	1.8
Dutch	2.7	1.8
Polish	3.7	1.2
Aboriginal	2.0	0.9
Italian	0.3	1.5
Russian	2.7	0.3
Asian	0.5	0.4
Austrian	1.4	0.3
Finnish	0.3	0.8
Other European	3.1	1.6
Other unclassified	0.2	0.3

that applied to American and British settlers as well as those from farther away. At the time of the 1931 Census, for example, 76.6 per cent of the Ontario population was Canadian-born compared to 66.2 per cent in Manitoba, 65.4 per cent in Saskatchewan, and 58.2 per cent in Alberta.[14] The prairie population was thus less thoroughly socialized into the norms and conventions of Canadian politics, or at least central Canadian politics. As W.L. Martin, Saskatchewan's Liberal premier at the end of World War I stated, "the people of this section of the country are principally settlers from the British Isles and the United States [who] have never known eastern Canada, and . . . stubbornly hold to the view that the West is Canada."[15] This view, alas, never took hold outside the West.

The immigrant base and ethnic complexity of the Prairies complicated the region's relationship with the federal government and national community. This, however, was only part of the problem:

The West was filled with a new polyglot population holding to a multitude of different religious creeds. It was a population, moreover, with shallow social roots, supplied with only the makeshift social institutions of early settlement, and facing an uncertain and frequently precarious economy. The problems of social integration were immense. To the extent that a distinctive regional society existed in western Canada it was perhaps born as much from the struggle with internal problems of integration and assimilation as it was from the struggle with the national government and eastern Canada.[16]

It was that latter struggle, however, that left the deepest imprint on western alienation. For a substantial part of the regional population, the political lessons learned through the rigors of agrarian settlement were written on a clear slate. There was no in-built attachment to the political status quo, no belief that the inherited traditions of parliamentary democracy were necessarily the best, or that the national political parties were owed any familial loyalty. To the extent that political slates were not clean, they carried messages from afar, from the populist movements in the United States and the Labour party in Britain, and from the traumas of central European politics.

The Grain Economy

The early regional economy in the prairie West was overwhelmingly based on grain produced for export to distant foreign (primarily European) markets. This wheat economy supported a unique regional way of life[17] and provided a mainstay of the national economy:

> As the annual wheat crop moved from the western farm to the loading ports of the east it served to justify an expensive system of transcontinental railroads, while the proceeds of its sale enabled the farmer in the West both to buy eastern manufactures, which in turn became the westbound traffic on the railroads, and to pay

for the financial services offered him by banks, grain traders, and mortgage companies. *Almost the whole Canadian economy was vitally affected by, and organized around, the movement of the annual grain crop into world markets* (emphasis added).[18]

The movement into world markets, however, was anything but smooth as the regional economy confronted a host of challenges and uncertainties.

Crop yields were subject to the vagaries of the erratic and frequently harsh Canadian climate whereas market demand rested on independent climatic conditions in Europe and those countries, particularly the United States and Australia, that were competing with Canadian producers for export markets. Western farmers were thousands of miles away from buyers overseas who could only be reached through extensive marketing and transportation systems beyond their immediate control; hence, regional frustration with the "middlemen" who controlled those systems and, in the eyes of western farmers, often reaped excessive profits at the farmers' expense. Agricultural settlement was dependent on securing financial credit, and the debt was held by eastern Canadian financial institutions not particularly knowledgeable about or sympathetic to the highly variable conditions confronting western farmers. There was, then, a chronic dependency on forces beyond the control of those in the region — a dependency that clashed with the fierce spirit of self-reliance animating those who wrestled a living from the prairie soil.

The "boom and bust" character of the regional economy further exacerbated the inherent problems of distance from markets and frontier debt. Good crops and strong export markets could bring handsome rewards just as weak markets and poor crops due to early frost, grasshoppers, and/or drought could bring disaster overnight. To paraphrase the Henry Wadsworth Longfellow poem, when times were good — when markets were strong, the Canadian climate favourable, and interest rates low — they were very, very good, and when times were bad — when markets were weak, frosts came early, and credit was expensive — they were horrid. Even so, optimism never died completely. No matter how difficult things might be, they were bound to be better "next year."[19]

It is important to stress that many of the challenges faced by prairie farmers were beyond the control of the most sympathetic federal governments. Even with the best of will, Ottawa could not move the West closer to global markets, although the condition of the transportation infrastructure and regulated freight rates could certainly moderate the financial effects of distance. Nonetheless, standing between western farmers and international markets were a host of national programs and policies that did have an impact on regional prosperity. The federal government set the tariffs on imported goods and thereby affected many of the input costs for agricultural production, particularly the cost of farm machinery. Ottawa set both rail freight rates and the more general regulatory framework for the railways linking the West to international markets, as well as regulating the financial institutions upon which western Canadian farmers were dependent. By the late 1930s, the Canadian Wheat Board monopolized foreign grain sales; it was the marketing body through which prairie grain production had to move.

THE NATIONAL POLICY

In 1879, Sir John A. Macdonald's Conservative government brought in the National Policy, which remained the mainstay of Canadian macroeconomic policy to the end of World War II. The tariffs it imposed on imports were designed to shield Canadian manufacturers from foreign — primarily American — competition and to encourage foreign firms to establish branch plants in Canada behind the protection of the tariff wall. In the era before personal income taxes, tariffs also generated a substantial part of the federal government's tax revenues, revenues that helped finance a national rail system linking the West to central Canadian and foreign markets. The costs of the National Policy — higher prices for imported goods — were borne by Canadians no matter where they lived, whereas the benefits — employment in the nascent Canadian manufacturing industries — were regionally concentrated in the population centers of Ontario and Quebec. The National Policy did not dictate the

location of manufacturing activities in central Canada as locational decisions were driven primarily by market considerations. Nonetheless, the
outcome was one in which central Canada was the clear beneficiary. As
supporters of the Progressive Party argued in the early 1920s, the effect
of the National Policy was "20 per cent less for everything we sell and 20
per cent more for everything we buy."

There is little question that the tariff protections of the National Policy
helped promote the development of a Canadian manufacturing industry.
However, there is no doubt whatsoever that it also left a very sour taste in
the mouths of agricultural producers in the West. The adjective "national"
came to be associated with policies designed to assist manufacturing interests in central Canada, often at the direct expense of farmers in the West.
The National Policy in 1879 and the National Energy Program in 1980
served to bracket and exemplify more than a century of public policies in
which western regional interests were sacrificed on the altar of a very
narrowly defined national interest.

One of the primary frustrations encountered by western Canadian
agricultural and natural resource producers stemmed from the inherent
inability of the federal government to protect export-based industries.
Tariffs, the basic instrument of national economic policy in the late nineteenth and early twentieth centuries, nurtured and protected the emer-
gent manufacturing industry in Ontario and Quebec by increasing the
price of imported goods to the point where domestic producers could
compete, perhaps at an advantage, with imported products. However,
tariffs could not be used to open up international markets for Canadian
crops or for that matter softwood lumber or other natural resources sold
on continental and global markets. As a consequence, western farmers
and natural resource producers more generally competed without tariff
protection on international markets while paying the additional input
costs that tariff protection imposed on the internal market. (This placed
prairie farmers at a particular disadvantage with American farmers just
south of the border.) Ottawa's hands may have been tied with respect to
opening up foreign markets, but this did little to reduce regional oppo-

sition to Canadian tariff policy and the costs it imposed on the regional economy — *costs* not *offset by regional benefits*. As a consequence, western Canadians were strong advocates of free or at least freer trade — a position less frequently advocated in Canada's manufacturing heartland.

The critical test for western Canadians was how well Ottawa performed in those areas where it did have some capacity to act, such as transportation policy and the regulation of financial institutions. Here it is fair to say that national policies were mixed. The introduction of the Crow Rate, which capped the freight rates on unprocessed grain moving out of the prairies, was certainly supported throughout most of the twentieth century, as was the establishment of the Canadian Wheat Board. More generally, however, and perhaps unfairly, the actions of the federal government were viewed as exploitative rather than supportive of the West. They were seen to reflect the financial, transportation, and manufacturing interests of Montreal and Toronto more than the interests of prairie homesteaders.

This, then, was the economic and political legacy left by the wheat economy that so dominated the prairie economy during the early decades of the twentieth century. Interestingly, this legacy continued to frame the regional political culture long after the grain economy lost its grip. In fact, it continues to do so today. As the primary motors of the regional economy shifted more to oil, natural gas, and petrochemicals in Alberta, and to a diversified resource base in the other western provinces, there was still a pervasive assumption that national policies were skewed in favour of the central Canadian provinces. Thus, relatively minor events, such as the federal government's 1986 decision to award the CF-18 maintenance contract to a Montreal firm despite a technically superior bid from a Winnipeg firm,[20] took on a great political profile. As Pat Burns, hotline radio host for Vancouver's CJOR, observed at the time of the CF-18 decision:

> Despite the fact that the Winnipeg-based Bristol Aerospace put in
> a lower bid and had a track record to show they were superior,

Canadair, in Montreal, ended up with the more-than-one-billion-dollar contract to service the CF-18 fighter planes Canada is buying from the United States. Quebec was superior in only one aspect. It has 75 federal seats, Manitoba 14. That and that alone is what got the contract for Canadair.[21]

In effect, the experiences of the wheat economy, writ large in regional scope and long in time, became the past and contemporary experience of the West as a whole. New events simply gave additional substance to an old story. Although in some cases western Canadians exaggerated the negative impact of national policies on regional prosperity, this is beside the point. Fact is no match for mythology in framing regional political cultures, in the West or elsewhere.

It should also be noted that although economic grievances lay at the core of regional discontent, such discontent could not be boiled down to economic grievances alone. They were reinforced by a cultural divide between "city mouse" and "country mouse," between "yeomen farmers" tilling the soil and "effete" central Canadians profiting, and at times profiteering, from their labour. These stereotypes—and they certainly were that—played to agrarian sensibilities in the early part of the twentieth century when political protest in the West expressed a strong anti-metropolitan sentiment. The Farmer's Platform in 1910, for example, stated that "the greatest misfortune that can befall any country is to have its people huddled together in great centers of population."[22] The reference to Toronto and Montreal was implicit but unmistakable.

The reality of regional stereotypes, of course, depended very much on where you stood. Still, it is undeniable that the stereotypes existed, that they reinforced economic conflict, and that they rippled through national politics. There is also no question that they persisted long after the rural/urban distinction between the West and central Canada had waned to the point of insignificance. The emerging western Canadian society was often seen from the outside as rustic, bucolic, and uncultured, lacking the sophistication of the Canadian heartland. The multicultural and multilingual immigrant experience of the West was contrasted unfavourably with the bicultural and bilingual national visions championed by other regions of the country. Western Canadian grievances were often portrayed as being simply about money and therefore were not given the same weight as the loftier concerns that Quebecers had about culture and language, that Atlantic Canadians had about the survival of traditional communities, and that the Toronto media had about the survival of a distinctive Canadian culture, based in Toronto. To quote former Prime Minister Joe Clark:

> [The] question of identity, the question of writers, is of great inter-
> est [in the West] because there is a common view that, in addition
> to everything else, Quebec is an artistic place, with a sense of real
> culture and real identity. I think people would scoff a little bit at
> the idea of there being a sense of culture and identity here. And
> yet there is a sense of culture and identity here, certainly not iden-
> tical to that in Quebec, certainly with different origins, perhaps
> even with different influence over the community. But part of the
> issue here is that the Quebec sense gets taken seriously, and the
> western sense does not.[23]

Thus, in a number of respects, western Canadians felt like outsiders in a country that they had done so much to build. The nationalist impulse that ran so strongly through the pioneer society, the desire to leave a positive mark on the national society, was rebuffed, not embraced, outside the region.

The interface between the grain economy and public policy, spiced by cultural conflict, led western Canadians in the early part of the last century to conclude that the source of agrarian grievances was to be found not so much in specific national policies as in the political system that produced such policies in the first place. The root cause lay with the political process itself rather than with the symptomatic nature of national policies that failed to reflect regional interests and aspirations.

This explanation retains its force to this day. But *why* was the political system tipped against the West? The answers to this question go well beyond the democratic impact of population disparities to a much more comprehensive regional critique of the Canadian political system.

ISOLATIONISM IN BRITISH COLUMBIA

The city mouse/country mouse cultural divide did not play out with as much strength in British Columbia where the agrarian community was much smaller and less homogeneous. To the extent that internal distinctions existed or exist, they were felt most strongly between those who lived in the "cultured" lower mainland and those who lived in the "uncultured" interior of the province. The more powerful schism in the "far West" or the "West beyond the West" was along the continental divide separating British Columbia from the rest, a divide reflecting the raw power of physical distance and geographic isolation from the Canadian heartland. Although that power has waned in the face of inexpensive and instantaneous electronic communications and ready air transportation, its impact on the regional political culture persists.

The Regional Critique

The West's critique of national policies and the national political system from which those policies sprang was wide-ranging and sparked a vigorous political response that has shaped the West's relationship with the broader national community from the early days of agrarian settlement to the present. However, just as the critique was expansive, so too was the political response, which was dispersed and dissipated across a wide assortment of targets — individual parties and leaders, the party system, financial institutions, federalism, parliamentary institutions, and Quebec. It has been, moreover, a remarkably unsuccessful response, given that the West, now as in the past, contains nearly a third of the national population. Despite this demographic weight, significant change has not occurred. While a century of regional protest has not left the national political system untouched, neither has it fundamentally altered the basic parameters of Canadian political life. And, in a circular fashion, failure has reinforced western perceptions that the political system is incapable of reflecting western Canadian concerns, values, and aspirations. It is important, therefore, to untangle the elements of the regional critique and to understand where it has found, and where it has failed to find, some traction on broader national debates about the nature of democratic politics in Canada.

Party Politics

For western Canadians on the agrarian frontier, the first explanation for discriminatory national policies lay with national political parties whose policy direction was set by transportation, banking, and manufacturing interests in central Canada — the very interests for whom the National Policy was crafted. This regional concentration of wealth and business reinforced the demographic dominance of Ontario and Quebec, thus fostering parties that were indifferent at best to the interests of western Canada. Not surprisingly, therefore, it was the national political parties, the Liberals and the Conservatives (who did not become Progressive until 1943), that took the first volley of regional discontent. Not surprisingly, because those parties carried the banner of financial and business interests and were on the front lines as the embryonic Canadian political system engaged settler communities in the West. The national parties also had relatively shallow roots in the West's immigrant population, which was infused with populist and nonpartisan ideas from American agrarian communities. Those ideas in turn had fostered a spirit of nonpartisanship both in the Territorial Assembly and in agrarian organizations.

How, then, did the western Canadian electorate respond? It is difficult, of course, to capture a century of complex electoral politics in a few paragraphs. Nonetheless, if we paint with a very broad brush, the outlines of a picture emerge. The first response of the regional electorate was to reject the Conservatives, the party most closely associated with the National Policy, and to support the federal Liberals, the party most closely associated with free trade and the immigration boom that began in the 1890s. (In British Columbia, where the National Policy had less bite, the Conservatives soldiered on with considerably more success than they achieved on the Prairies.) With western Canadian and particularly Saskatchewan support, the Liberals under Sir Wilfrid Laurier formed a string of national governments from 1896 to 1911. The second response, in 1917 and especially in 1921, was to reject both parties in favour of nonpartisanship and a regionally-based, agrarian populist movement embodied in the Progressive Party of Canada[24] (not to be confused with the Conservatives, who were still not Progressive). Following the Progressive revolt in 1921 came nearly four decades (1925-57) of electoral trench warfare in the West between the Liberals, on the one hand, and the Cooperative Commonwealth Federation (CCF), the Alberta-based Social Credit party, and remnants of the Progressive Party, on the other. Throughout this period the prairie West remained a Conservative wasteland, a situation that did not change in 1943 when the party acquired the moniker but not the electoral support of the Progressive movement by renaming itself the Progressive Conservative Party of Canada.

Dramatic change came in 1958 when the Progressive Conservatives, now led by maverick Saskatchewan lawyer John Diefenbaker, enlarged a 1957 minority government foothold in Ontario and Atlantic Canada to sweep the West and the rest of the country. Diefenbaker's Conservatives won 209 of 265 seats in the House of Commons, the greatest proportionate victory in the history of the House.[25] As Denis Smith explains:

He gave to the Prairies for the first time in their history the same sense of dynamic and central participation in nation-building that his predecessor, John A. Macdonald, had given to central Canada after 1867 . . . [his policies] were policies of national integration that typified the prairie conception of Canada.[26]

The partisan transformation in the West, however, came not because the Conservatives swept the West — they swept the whole country, including Quebec — but because, as the rest of the country drifted back to the Liberals in subsequent elections, the West stayed Tory blue. There was a brief flirtation in 1968 with the Trudeau Liberals, who won 27 of 68 regional seats, but by and large, and particularly in Alberta, the region remained a Conservative stronghold. As a consequence, western Canadian MPs largely found themselves on the opposition side of the House when the Liberals formed national governments in the 1965, 1968, 1972, 1974, and 1980 elections. This exclusion from the national government undoubtedly fanned the coals of western alienation.

The West came on board the winning side in 1984, not because the region finally abandoned a losing cause but because Brian Mulroney's Progressive Conservatives swept the country, including the West, in a manner reminiscent of Diefenbaker's triumph in 1958. In effect, the national government came to the West rather than western Canadians shifting their partisan allegiances. Under Mulroney, western MPs were firmly entrenched in the national government, with western ministers such as Don Mazankowski and Joe Clark exercising considerable power. However, regional satisfaction with the Conservative government was short-lived, and 1987 saw the creation of the Reform Party of Canada with its mandate "the West wants in." After a false start in the 1988 election, which was dominated by the proposed Free Trade Agreement with the United States, an issue on which Reform and the Progressive Conservative government saw eye to eye, Reform and then the Canadian Alliance went on to dominate the West, winning 67 per cent of the regional seats across the three federal elections of 1993, 1997, and 2000.

One conclusion is emphatically clear from this brief synopsis of partisanship in the West: a variety of strategies — supporting the Liberals, supporting the Conservatives, supporting neither, and creating new, regionally based parties — have all failed in getting sufficient regional leverage on Parliament. For most of the past century, and carrying

FALL FROM GRACE

Brian Mulroney's fall from grace in western Canada was dramatic. Initially, his government phased out the NEP and replaced it with the Western Energy Accord; legislated the Western Canadian Grain Stabilization Fund; created the department of Western Economic Diversification; and, through the Free Trade Agreement, delivered on a policy that western Canadians had been advocating for generations. Western MPs were prominent players in the Progressive Conservative cabinets, and the majority of western MPs were finally on the government side of the House; the Conservatives captured 75.3 per cent of the region's seats in 1984 and 55.8 per cent in 1988. Then, in 1993 the Conservatives were wiped out in the West and have made very little recovery since. In part, the explanation has nothing to do with the West per se; it may simply have been a national tidal wave that swept aside the Conservatives. However, the Mulroney experience also shows the depth of western alienation and the extent of estrangement from the national government; even strong regional representation within the national government is not sufficient to assuage a sense of alienation anchored by generations of adverse experience. Certainly this was the case with respect to the Mulroney government's CF-18 decision, which sent a strong message that it was business as usual in Ottawa. There is also little question that Mulroney's advocacy of a special constitutional status for Quebec played out poorly in the West, as did his failure to address the deficit financing of the previous Liberal governments. Cabinet representation accomplishes little if the perception is that ministers are representing Ottawa to the West rather than the West to Ottawa.

forward into the start of the twenty-first century, the majority of western MPs have found themselves on the Opposition side of the House of Commons. As Figure 2.2 shows, in the 18 general elections held since the end of World War II, western Canadian constituencies have elected MPs to the government side of the House only 37.5 per cent of the time. Other regions, particularly Ontario, have had much better track records. Here the comparison with Quebec is particularly interesting. Despite widespread and prolonged nationalist discontent in Quebec reaching back to the end of the war, the Quebec electorate still sent a majority of its MPs to the government side of the House. Quebec MPs, therefore, generally sat with the government of the day, whereas western Canadian MPs generally sat on the opposition benches. It is no small wonder that discontent with parliamentary politics has been much more pronounced in the West, where the propensity to vote for the losing side is unmatched elsewhere in the country.

FIGURE 2.2: GOVERNMENT AND OPPOSITION MPS, 1945–2000

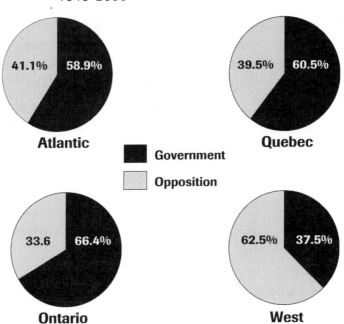

The current situation, in which a regional block of Canadian Alliance MPs squares off across the floor of the House with a Liberal government, is far from exceptional. Given the grip of party discipline in the House, this outcome means that the majority of western MPs have had *no* effective influence on national policy. It is not surprising, therefore, that national policy often runs counter to regional interests in the West. After all, it has been policy forged by MPs from other regions with other regional axes to grind.

It appears that the West can contribute to "throwing the bastards out," can help bring some of the old bastards back in, or can create new bastards altogether, but no option seems to result in national treatment that is fair and equitable or, at least, is seen as such. As a consequence, the regional critique turned to the more fundamental reform of party politics, federalism, and parliamentary institutions.

Populism

The failure of partisan strategies in the West helps explain the appeal of populism and direct democracy. If the parties could not be trusted as intermediaries between the regional electorate and the policy processes of the federal government, then populism's appeal could only grow. Giving power to the people directly through referendums or plebiscites is a way to bypass both the parties and the parliamentary institutions in which they are embedded.

Populism has deep roots within western Canada.[27] It grew out of the perception that external elites were exploiting the region, that the political system was tilted away from the people at large and towards those few holding economic wealth and power. As Sydney Sharpe and Don Braid explain, "populism is a western tradition because of the frustration people feel towards a perceived colonial power structure in Ottawa."[28] This frustration was fed by regional representation in the House of Commons where western MPs, even if and perhaps especially if elected to the government side of the House, became so entangled in partisan interests and constraints that voters back home were forgotten or ignored. Therefore, a way was sought to make MPs more responsible to their constituents and less beholden to national parties based in Ontario and Quebec or, if that failed, to bypass the party system completely. Thus, we saw the early appeal to nonpartisanship and direct democracy in order to put power in the hands of "the people."[29] While populism is not without appeal in other parts of the country, there is no question that it has been much stronger in the West than elsewhere.

The strongest advocate of populism in recent years was the Reform Party of Canada, which pledged, for better or for worse, to respect "the common sense of the common people," and it is difficult to imagine a better nutshell description of populism than that.

THE POPULIST SPIRIT

David Kilgour, Liberal MP for Edmonton Southeast, nicely captures the contemporary populist spirit in western Canada:

"Most of our parents and grandparents, or a lot of them, went out and broke the land, and we inherited a lot of their attitudes. We like frugality; we believe in cooperation; we believe in public health care — a whole lot of things this region has contributed to Canada. We do not believe in elite accommodation. We believe in a populist sort of democracy where everybody is equal; we don't look for elites to accommodate. This is one of the reasons western Canada is very special: We've tried to democratize Canada, whether it's the Senate or whatever, and we will continue to try to democratize Canada."[30]

Populism fits neatly within the broader context of western alienation; it has intuitive appeal to people who see themselves victimized by distant economic and political elites with little understanding of or sympathy for the "grass roots." Through the tools of direct democracy, populism seeks to bridge the gulf between the rulers and the ruled, a gulf that for western Canadians has always existed in at least a geographic sense. (Westerners are quick to refer to the "Ottawa disease," an affliction that overcomes western MPs as soon as they arrive in Ottawa by wiping out any memory of regional concerns or empathy for regional interests.) As former Leader of the Official Opposition Preston Manning writes:

Whenever populism has become a force to be reckoned with in Western Canadian politics, it has been energized by "western alienation" — a conviction shared by generations of Western Canadians that their region and interests have not achieved equality with the constitutional and economic interests of Quebec and Ontario, and that systemic change is necessary to achieve such equality.[31]

In short, populism has been part of the West's response to the regional political critique sketched in above. It became an important feature of a regional political culture shaped around the themes of western alienation. However, it is by no means the full story.

Federalism

Since federalism permeates virtually every nook and cranny of Canadian political life, we might expect that the West's regional critique would have had federalism in its sights from the get-go. This was not the case. Federalism, and more specifically the federal division of powers, was not an initial or primary target for western Canadian discontent. In part this was because the powers of government that were of immediate interest to western Canada during the period of agricultural settlement could not easily be devolved to the provinces. It did not make sense to give provincial legislatures powers over tariffs, international trade, interprovincial transportation, or national financial management, and yet it was precisely these powers that potentially determined regional prosperity. The essential need, therefore, was for more effective policy influence in Ottawa rather than for a devolution of powers to the provinces. Thus the Reform Party called first and foremost for the West's inclusion — "the West wants in" — rather than for a substantial decentralization of the Canadian federal state.

The West's federalism agenda with respect to the division of powers has been modest and defensive in character. The initial goal was to ensure that the prairie provinces enjoyed the same ownership of natural resources exercised by other provinces — a goal achieved by the 1930 *Natural*

Resources Transfer Act. In subsequent decades there was little impetus, and certainly no concerted action, for change in the division of powers. The Social Credit government in Alberta did initially push the federalism envelope in the late 1930s with unsuccessful legislative initiatives relating to banking and censorship of the press, but this was offset by the western-based CCF's support for stronger national powers with respect to economic management and social policy. For the first 70 years of the twentieth century, western Canadians and their governments made at best sporadic attempts to link the federal division of powers to regional discontent. Federalism in this respect was neither the problem nor the solution.

CONTRASTING FEDERAL VISIONS IN QUEBEC AND THE WEST

The federalism perspectives of Quebec and the West have converged in some respects and diverged in others. Both regions have resented and resisted federal government intrusions into provincial fields of jurisdiction, and in this sense both have been defenders of the constitutional status quo. (As the contemporary debate on health policy illustrates, some provinces, particularly Saskatchewan, have been less resistant to federal intrusions than have others.) The goal was to respect and protect provincial powers. However, Quebec governments since the early 1960s have also sought expansion of the provincial legislative domain, an objective not pursued with any great enthusiasm by provincial governments in the West. More fundamental divergences have occurred on two fronts. First, Quebec's quest for constitutional recognition as a distinct society has no counterpart in the West, where the constitutional ideal has been defined by the equality of provinces. Second, the West's quest for the reform of parliamentary institutions has found no support in Quebec apart from a shared interest in how appointments are made to the Supreme Court. Hence, the emergence of very different federal visions in the two regions. For Quebecers — speaking very generally indeed! — the ideal vision is a more decentralized federalism with parliamentary institutions left pretty much intact. For western Canadians, the vision includes radically reformed parliamentary institutions with the division of powers left pretty much intact, but more faithfully respected.

This situation had potential for change in the mid-1960s when nationalists of all stripes in Quebec began a concerted drive to enhance the legislative powers exercised by the Quebec National Assembly. (Some took this to the extreme of advocating independence, while others sought a more autonomous Quebec within Canada.) However, this crusade was not supported with any great enthusiasm by western provincial governments, nor did western Canadians at large support a substantially more decentralized federal state. The support that did exist probably reflected generalized discontent with the federal governments of the day more than principled commitment to greater decentralization. True, the West had been changing in many ways and to an extent that rivaled the Quiet Revolution in Quebec. The regional economy was more diversified, markets for natural resources were robust, OPEC had driven up the price for oil and natural gas, immigration into the region had resumed following the demographic disaster of the Great Depression, the West's share of the national population was increasing again after four decades of decline, and cities across the region were booming. Yet, despite these changes, the region's constitutional stance remained relatively constant. In the negotiations leading up to the 1982 Constitution Act, the western premiers, led by Alberta's Peter Lougheed, primarily sought to shore up constitutional protection for the provincial ownership of natural resources. This defensive stance, which was successful, was not accompanied by any demand for a redistribution of legislative responsibilities. The basic stance towards this dimension of federalism was to stand pat and to ward off federal intrusions into existing fields of provincial responsibility.

If the reform impulse in western Canada did not generate a call for a change in the federal division of powers, it did create a barrage of criticism about how Ottawa exercised its existing legislative responsibilities. Western Canadians focused on the federal lack of respect for the division of powers and a willingness by the federal government to use its spending power to intrude into provincial areas of responsibility. The western stance, therefore, was again defensive in character, calling for greater respect for the constitutional status quo. However, the logic of this critique also opened up a debate on institutional reform. If the West's principal concern was how Ottawa exercised its powers, and if there was no widespread political support for limiting Ottawa's constitutional field of action, that logic called for change in the way in which national institutions conducted the affairs of state. Hence the regional drive for Senate reform and, more generally, for a set of parliamentary institutions capable of handling the contemporary demands of governance in a complex federal society.

Parliamentary Reform

Parties and the governments they cobble together do not operate in a vacuum, and it was inevitable that the regional critique would extend eventually to the institutional framework of Canadian political life. Here the conclusion is depressingly similar to those stemming from a regional analysis of the party system: parliamentary institutions compound the regional effects embedded in the country's demography. In short, parliamentary institutions make a bad situation worse by exacerbating rather than moderating regional conflict. The critique of parliamentary institutions applies with particular force to the federal character of those institutions.

Federalism entails more than the division of legislative responsibilities between two constitutionally defined orders of government. It also entails institutional principles with respect to how citizens are represented and how decisions are made *within* national legislatures. In the United States, the prototypical federal system, citizens are represented nationally on the basis of population — one person, one vote — in the House of Representatives while their state of residence is equally represented in the Senate, with each state having two and only two Senators regardless of the state's population. (California, with nearly 30,000,000 residents, has two Senators, as does Montana with only 800,000 residents.) Therefore, "rep-by-pop" in the House is counterbalanced by "rep-by-territory" in the Senate. In a similar fashion, Australia combines representation by population in the House of Representatives with equal state representation — in this instance, 12 Senators per state — in the Senate. In both the American and Australian cases, Senators are directly elected by the people of their states. Bicameralism, the existence of two legislative chambers with different representational bases and constitutionally defined powers, is an essential, indeed defining characteristic of federal states. Or so one would think from surveying the international community.

REGIONAL REPRESENTATION IN THE CANADIAN SENATE

In 1867, Canada opted for equal regional representation in the Senate rather than equal provincial representation. However, two of the regions — Ontario and Quebec — were in fact provinces, and each received 24 Senators. The maritime provinces also received a regional allocation of 24 seats, divided into 12 each for New Brunswick and Nova Scotia, and then divided again when Prince Edward Island became a province to give 10 seats each to New Brunswick and Nova Scotia, and four to PEI. The West eventually became a senatorial region with 24 seats, six for each of the western provinces. When Newfoundland joined confederation, it received six seats, and the three northern territories now have one Senator each. The resulting configuration of Senate seats is a dog's breakfast bereft of any logic relating to either rep-by-pop or rep-by-territory. It is tolerated only because the Senate is seen by Canadians as irrelevant to their lives.

Canada stands apart from other federal states in that we have a *de facto unicameral* national parliament dominated overwhelmingly by the House of Commons. The Senate makes a mockery of federal principles. Senators are neither elected by citizens nor appointed by provincial governments; they are appointed at the sole discretion of the prime minister and retain their seats until reaching 75 years of age. The number of Senate seats per province is based on the math of

Confederation, which bears little resemblance to today's demographic or federal realities. If we try to impose the logic of representation by population on the Senate, recognizing that provincial equality has never been in play, Table 2.2 shows that the status quo becomes even more peculiar; British Columbia and Alberta are the most under-represented provinces in the Senate. The Senate has no electoral mandate and no democratic legitimacy. It is based on neither representation by population nor equal representation for territorial communities. It fails, moreover, to exercise significant legislative independence from the House of Commons, and therefore provides no effective check on the federal cabinet. Senators are accountable to no one for the actions they take, or fail to take. From the perspective of federalism or regional representation, the Senate can most charitably be described as wasted institutional space.[32] While this conclusion is not meant to discredit the performance and public service of individual Senators, the existing Senate is impossible to defend on the basis of federal or democratic principles. It is an institution poorly designed for the nineteenth century, much less the twenty-first.

Just as it was inevitable that the quest for a more effective regional voice within the corridors of power in Ottawa would become a quest for a more effective *institutional* voice, it was equally inevitable that this latter quest would focus on the Senate. Perhaps the only surprise is that Senate reform is a relative newcomer to the regional critique. The Senate as a target for regional discontent dates largely from the constitutional debates of the 1970s and 1980s. This is not to say that the Senate was ever popular, for it was not, either in the West or elsewhere. Until comparatively recently, however, Senate reform was not commonly seen as a potential solution for regional grievances. In short, the Senate had a very low profile in the West as it did elsewhere in Canada. This situation changed when Canada's constitutional debate broke open with the election of the Parti Québecois government in 1976. At that time, the country's entire constitutional and institutional framework, including the Senate, was placed on the negotiating table.

TABLE 2.2:   PROVINCIAL REPRESENTATION IN THE CANADIAN SENATE

PROVINCE/ TERRITORY	NUMBER OF SENATORS	POPULATION PER SENATOR
Newfoundland	6	85,000
Prince Edward Island	4	34,000
Nova Scotia	10	91,000
New Brunswick	10	73,000
Quebec	24	302,000
Ontario	24	475,000
Manitoba	6	187,000
Saskatchewan	6	163,000
Alberta	6	496,000
British Columbia	6	651,000
Yukon	1	29,000
Northwest Territories	1	37,000
Nunavut	1	27,000
Canada	**105**	**286,000**

In today's environment, it is difficult to discuss western alienation without immediately bringing into play Senate reform. Support for Senate reform, and more particularly the call for a Triple E Senate — equal, elected, and effective — is a staple of western Canadian political discourse, often joined with proposals for electoral and parliamentary reform. Western Canadians strongly support Senate reform, and their support waxes and wanes little in response to differences in provincial residency, income, age, sex, or even partisanship. Nor, for that matter, has it changed much over time.

Although the Senate provides the contemporary focus for the western Canadian institutional critique, the House of Commons has not escaped critical comment. As Table 2.3 illustrates, the House does not come close to representation by population, at least as calculated on a regional basis. Not surprisingly, the two provinces with the greatest degree of under-representation at the present time are Alberta and

FIGURE 2.3:   REGIONAL SUPPORT FOR SENATE REFORM
("The Senate Should be Equal and Elected")

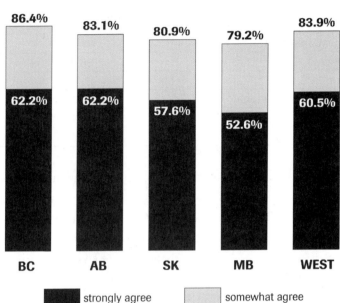

Source: Berdahl

British Columbia, albeit followed closely by Ontario. On other fronts, the iron grip of party discipline across all aspects of the House has made it next to impossible for western MPs, or indeed any MPs, to stand up publicly for regional interests should such interests conflict with partisan majorities, generally anchored in Ontario and Quebec. Canadians are told that vigorous regional representation takes place within party caucuses and around the cabinet table, but if such representation does take place, it takes place behind closed doors and out of sight. (In the case of the cabinet, secrecy is assured through the potential penalties of the Official Secrets Act.) Justice not seen to be done is seldom perceived as justice done, and the argument that the system in fact works "if only you could see what takes place behind closed doors" carries little weight.

To summarize briefly, western Canadians are not convinced that parliamentary institutions as currently designed provide effective

TABLE 2.3:   POPULATION REPRESENTED BY MPS, 2001
              CENSUS[33]

	POPULATION PER MP
Atlantic Canada	71,000
Quebec	96,000
Ontario	111,000
Manitoba/Saskatchewan	75,000
Alberta	115,000
British Columbia	114,000

regional representation. Admittedly, this conclusion has not always been part of the regional critique; in a 1949 speech to the House of Commons, John Diefenbaker said "No Canadian can but be proud that through the warp and woof of our Constitution are the golden threads of our British Heritage."[34] Diefenbaker was not a fan of institutional reform. Today, however, there is a broad regional consensus that Canada's parliamentary institutions — our "British Heritage"—are not up to the demands and expectations of governance in the twenty-first century. Interestingly, a similar conclusion has been reached in the United Kingdom where the House of Lords (the equivalent of and inspiration for our Senate) has been radically reformed, new legislative institutions have been created for Scotland and Wales, and the merits of electoral reform are being hotly debated. Only in Canada is it assumed that parliamentary institutions should be immune to changing social conditions and democratic expectations.

The western Canadian critique has the potential to contribute to a broader democratic reform debate in Canada. The regional critique, for instance, begins to merge with and reinforce a more general democratic concern with prime ministerial dominance (and the analogous dominance of premiers within provincial governments), the secretive character of decision-making, and the impotent role of individual MPs and parliamentary committees. To date, however, the fusion of regional discontent and national democratic discontent has been at best fitful and incomplete. Indeed, regional support for democratic reform may even contribute to the implacable opposition of successive national governments to democratic reform. If western Canadians support democratic reform, it must be a suspect idea!

Western Alienation as a Regional Political Culture

The facts that western alienation is deeply rooted in the regional community and that it reflects much more than an itemized list of policy grievances suggest that it is best conceptualized as an integral part of the West's political culture. By this we mean that western alienation is a learned predisposition, that its basic tenets are pervasively shared, and that it is not easily dislodged or eroded by changes in specific public policies or political leadership. Of course, this is not to say that the political culture in the West can be reduced to alienation alone. It is also infused by liberal democratic values held across the country, and western Canadians are thoroughly engaged with a broad range of policy issues for which western alienation cannot provide a frame — genetic engineering, educational reform, humanitarian aid, defence policy, industrial productivity, and Aboriginal peoples are just part of a long list. At the same time, however, the political culture in the West is distinctive, and its distinctiveness comes from the contribution of western alienation.

One of the puzzles to people outside the region is how alienation is often fanned rather than subdued by prosperity. Here Alberta provides a striking example; peaks of discontent appear to coincide with peaks in economic prosperity. This situation is contrasted to the situation in Atlantic Canada, where discontent appears to be driven more by regional disparities. This in turn leads to the perception that western alienation is little more than bitching and whining by people who are well off, and therefore it can be dismissed.

There is, needless to say, some discontent within Alberta over the perceived costs of Confederation. Note, for example, a 2001 editorial in the *Calgary Herald*:

In 1998, Alberta dished out $5.7 billion more than it received; by contrast Quebec swallowed $5.9 billion more than it paid. While Quebecers benefited $797 per person from Confederation, Albertans paid out $1,955 each. As Alberta's have-economy expands, so do the demands of the country. Alberta Treasury calculates that the net loss to Albertans grew to $2,651 per person in 1999, and $2,905 in 2000. Albertans wouldn't begrudge the financial imbalance; helping one's neighbour is a value that thrives in the West. It's just that a little appreciation is long overdue.[35]

At the same time, however, there is a critically important linkage of western alienation to future aspirations, to the determination to ensure regional prosperity for generations to come. The fear is that national policies may limit the future capacity and prosperity of the West.

It should also be noted that western alienation is often seen to be targeted at Quebec, and thus the accusation is made that the regional political culture is deeply and unfortunately impregnated with hostility towards Quebec and towards French Canada more broadly defined. Like all stereotypes, this one has some elements of truth. The settlement experience in the West gave little support for bilingual and bicultural models for Canada, and respect for minority language rights was historically seen as an impediment to the assimilation of a large, polyglot immigrant population. Western Canadians have reacted with a great deal of hostility to the attempts of Quebec nationalists to break up a country that western Canadians did so much to build, and there has been resentment about Quebec's lock since 1968 on the country's national leadership. As mentioned above, even federalists within Quebec have pursued a constitutional vision considerably at odds with that favoured by the majority of western Canadians. More generally, western Canadians believe that the West's interests have been ignored by a national government fixated on Quebec. Hence Diane Ablonczy's reference in this chapter's opening quotation to the "utter indifference" of the national government.

THE ROOTS OF WESTERN ALIENATION   61

There is also a broad belief that federal program spending is consistently skewed in favour of Quebec. In the words of Don Martin, Ottawa correspondent for the *Calgary Herald*, "the conventional and well-deserved western view of Ottawa has always been that of a giant money-laundering operation turning honest tax dollars into Quebec payola."[36] Or, in the more profane imagery of Ric Dolphin, Western Bureau Chief for the *Calgary Herald*, the first lesson in federal-provincial relations is that "Ottawa only wants the West for what it can pay. Quebec bats its eyes and Ottawa drops to its knees and ..."[37]

CONSTITUTIONAL PARADOX

There is an important irony in the constitutional battles of the past three decades. Nationalist discontent in Quebec drove the constitutional process, and the West largely reacted to a constitutional agenda set by Quebec. However, in most respects the constitutional outcomes, and particularly the *Constitution Act of 1982*, better reflected western Canadian political values than they did the constitutional values of Quebec. The amending formula embedded in the 1982 Act was written by the western premiers, and the Charter of Rights reflects liberal values deeply entrenched in the political culture of western Canada. The continuation of the status quo with respect to the division of powers also fits the constitutional inclinations of western Canadians. The major exception is the lack of any headway on Senate reform — a failure for which Quebec's opposition has played a decisive role. Nonetheless, although western Canadians have largely been bystanders to a constitutional game played out between opposing Quebec politicians based in Ottawa and Quebec City, the outcomes of that game have not been detrimental to the West.

So, there is no question that the two regions have chafed against one another throughout most of the last century. However, if we look at the contemporary environment, it is increasingly clear that western Canadians place less and less emphasis on their region's relationship with Quebec. The focus instead is on continental trade and global positioning. What goes on within Quebec is seen as irrelevant for the future of regional prosperity, with one important exception: Quebec's dominant position within the federal government may still play a decisive role in determining whether federal policies are ones that foster or impede prosperity in western Canada.

Conclusions

At the outset of this chapter we argued that western Canadians position themselves globally *through* Canada. Western Canadians therefore have a stake in a vital and united Canada, their portal to the global economy. This explains in part why western alienation is not at odds with a strong sense of Canadian nationalism, but is better seen as nationalism frustrated by the political system. However, the regional stake in Canada will remain in the future only if national policies retain their relevance by facilitating rather than constraining regional prosperity.

With respect to the first condition, things have indeed changed. In a free trade environment, and particularly within the context of NAFTA, western Canadian producers have direct access to American and global markets that is increasingly unmediated by the federal government. Grain farmers, for example, have Internet access to spot grain markets in a manner that calls into question the role of the Canadian Wheat Board. While rail, air, road, and sea transportation linkages between the West and global markets remain critically important, federal programs have less and less to do with such linkages — federal spending on transportation infrastructure has declined, airports have been privatized, and federal regulatory frameworks have largely given way to market competition. As a consequence of these changes, what Ottawa does or does not do has less capacity to assist or harm a regional economy characterized more and more by strong north-south ties and comparatively weaker east-west ties. While it would be a gross overstatement to say that Ottawa counts for naught, it does count for less. Whether this is a desirable state of affairs is an important question in its own right, but there is little doubt that the empirical reality, for better or for worse, points to a diminished federal role.

CRISIS OR OPPORTUNITY?

Joe Clark: "There's a deep-seated alienation in western Canada. . ... It takes the form sometimes of simply anti-system feeling, which is deeply rooted here. That's the minority part of it. I think there's also a significant sense of frustration that western Canadians are not able to have an impact upon — or think we're not able to have the impact upon the shaping of the nation. Is it a crisis? Not yet. I think it is a very significant opportunity for a national government."[38]

Finally, and perhaps more importantly, the verdict is still out on whether remaining national programs are of net benefit to western Canada as the region adjusts to new economic realities. In the past, people came to the West because of the richness of the soil and the vast stock of natural resources. In today's knowledge-based economy, firms and individuals have less need to locate near resources; thus, the West's competitive advantage of the past will be less of an asset in the future. However, the capacity of the region to adjust to and thrive within this new economic environment will still be determined in part by public policies, including national public policies. It is therefore critically important to ask if such policies are crafted in a way that accommodates regional interests, addresses regional priorities, and promotes regional aspirations. Are the national and regional policy agendas aligned? Are federal programs still relevant for regional prosperity? Positive answers to these questions may well depend on finding a more effective regional voice for the West within the national government and national community.

Notes

1   "Western Alienation: A *This Morning* Roundtable," *Policy Options* (April 2001): 7.
2   "The West wants in" was the founding slogan of the Reform Party of Canada. Whatever one might think of Reform, there is no question that the slogan neatly captured a century of regional discontent.
3   "Western Alienation" 12-13.
4   Ilana Mercer, "Raise a toast to Western separatism and Canada's good health," *Globe and Mail* 3 January 2001: A11.
5   Peter Menzies, "Deregulation process needs stabilization," *Calgary Herald* 29 January 2001: A10.
6   A.R.M. Lower, *From Colony to Nation: A History of Canada* (Toronto, ON: Longmans, Green and Company, 1946).
7   Like Russian dolls, colonization models can also be applied to Canada's Aboriginal peoples, as was done by the Royal Commission on Aboriginal Peoples, and to the northern territories, which still lack formal provincial status and ownership of their natural resources.
8   The treatment of Aboriginal peoples is an important topic in its own right, but one that connects only tangentially to western alienation. The latter deals with the relationship between the settler community and the larger national community and its government. To fold the history of Aboriginal peoples into this framework would shed little light on the latter while providing an inappropriate vehicle for understanding the former.
9   Cited in Frank H. Underhill, *In Search of Canadian Liberalism* (Toronto, ON: Macmillan, 1960) 55.
10 Donald V. Smiley, *Canada in Question: Federalism in the Seventies*, 2nd ed. (Toronto, ON: McGraw-Hill, 1976) 193.
11 Vernon C. Fowke, *Canadian Agricultural Policy: The Historical Pattern* (Toronto, ON: University of Toronto Press, 1947) 177.
12 The phrase "the last, best west" was used in immigration promotional materials of the period. For a vivid pictorial history of this era, see Jean Bruce, *The Last Best West* (Toronto, ON: Fitzhenry and Whiteside, 1976).
13 Table adapted from Roger Gibbins, *Prairie Politics and Society: Regionalism in Decline* (Scarborough, ON: Butterworths, 1980) 20.
14 Gibbins, *Prairie Politics and Society* 22.
15 Cited in David E. Smith, *Prairie Liberalism: The Liberal Party in Saskatchewan, 1905-1971* (Toronto, ON: University of Toronto Press, 1975) 327-28.
16 Gibbins, *Prairie Politics and Society* 25.
17 Vernon C. Fowke, *The National Policy and the Wheat Economy* (Toronto, ON: University of Toronto Press, 1957) 282.
18 J.R. Mallory, *Social Credit and the Federal Power in Canada* (Toronto, ON: University of Toronto Press, 1953) 38.
19 Hence the title of Jean Burnet's history of Alberta, *Next Year Country: A Study of Rural Social Organization in Alberta* (Toronto, ON: University of Toronto Press, 1978).
20 For a detailed discussion of the CF-18 incident, see Robert M. Campbell and Leslie A. Pal, *The Real World of Canadian Politics: Cases in Process and Policy* (Peterborough, ON: Broadview Press, 1989) Chapter 1.
21 Pat Burns, on-air editorial for Vancouver's CJOR, 10 November 1986. Cited in *The Western Separatist Papers* 11, 9 (September 1993): 3.
22 David E. Smith, "Western Politics and National Unity," *Canada and the Burden of Unity*, ed. David Jay Bercuson (Toronto, ON: Macmillan, 1977) 144.
23 "Western Alienation" 12.
24 See W.L. Morton, *The Progressive Party in Canada* (Toronto, ON: University of Toronto Press, 1950).

[25] Brian Mulroney's Progressive Conservatives won more seats (211) in their 1984 landslide victory, but the House then had 282 rather than 265 seats.

[26] Denis Smith, "Liberals and Conservatives on the Prairies, 1917-1968," *Prairie Perspectives*, ed. David P. Gagan (Toronto, ON: Holt, Rinehart and Winston, 1970) 41.

[27] David Laycock, *Populism and Democratic Thought in the Canadian Prairies, 1910 — 1945* (Toronto, ON: University of Toronto Press, 1990).

[28] Sydney Sharpe and Don Braid, *Storming Babylon: Preston Manning and the Rise of the Reform Party* (Toronto, ON: Key Porter Books, 1992) 61.

[29] David Laycock, "Reforming Canadian Democracy? Institutions and Ideology in the Reform Party Project," *Canadian Journal of Political Science* 27 (June 1994).

[30] "Western Alienation" 9.

[31] Preston Manning, *The New Canada* (Toronto, ON: Macmillan, 1992) 119.

[32] For the classic but still applicable analysis of Senate reform, see Peter McCormick, Ernest C. Manning, and Gordon Gibson, *Regional Representation: The Canadian Partnership* (Calgary, AB: Canada West Foundation, 1981).

[33] *National Post*, 8 March 2002, A14.

[34] Cited in Margaret Wente, ed., *I Never Say Anything Provocative* (Toronto, ON: Peter Martin, 1975) 84.

[35] "What the West wants," *Calgary Herald* 27 January 2001: OS6.

[36] Don Martin, "Your tax dollars at work," *Calgary Herald* 7 May 2002: A 3.

[37] Ric Dolphin, "Welcome to tales from "Buffalo Trail,'" *Calgary Herald* 8 May 2002: A3.

[38] "Western Alienation" 7.

CHAPTER 3

WESTERN ALIENATION ON THE CONTEMPORARY LANDSCAPE

"In the West the seeds of alienation were planted early. The roots go deep. The West believes that Central Canada — Eastern Canada in Everyman's language — was the real beneficiary of Confederation. The Prairies are not grateful for the colonial heritage . . . there is a widespread feeling in the West that Eastern politicians, financiers and businessmen have no real understanding of conditions in the West and no real desire to learn."[1]

—J.A. ARCHER, historian

Introduction

The last chapter emphasized the historical continuity of regional discontent in western Canada. In the words of J.A. Archer, "the seeds were planted early" and "the roots go deep." Chapter 2 argued, therefore, that the pattern of alienation laid down during the early decades of agrarian settlement on the prairies is still evident today even though the demographic and economic profile of the West has been dramatically transformed. In short, the *attitudinal landscape* of the urban West in the early years of the twenty-first century, inclusive of British Columbia, reflects that of the agrarian West at the turn of the twentieth century. Thus, the analysis in Chapter 2 moved easily from the National Policy of 1879 to editorial commentary in 2002, from the challenges first encountered by the wheat economy to the National Energy Program (NEP) and the rise of the Reform Party. Throughout, the stress was on an overarching and integrating theme, "the West wants in," and the accompanying frustration that this aspiration had not been met.

Some readers, however, might protest at this point, saying "but what has the National Policy got to do with my life today, in a very different West?" Take a reader who is 21 when this book is first published in 2003, and imagine her at a coffee shop in Vancouver's West End, or having a beer at the Forks in Winnipeg:

- when the Reform Party was created in 1987, she would have been five years old;
- when the National Energy Program was introduced in 1980, she would not have been born and her *parents* would have been in their early twenties;
- when John Diefenbaker formed a majority national government in 1958, her *grandparents* would have been in their early twenties; and
- when the National Policy was introduced in 1879, her *great, great, great grandparents* would have been starting their family.

There is, then, something audacious in asserting a common pattern of political beliefs that stretches across this huge generational canvas, that links in a meaningful way the National Policy, freight rates, the NEP, and the policy challenges facing the contemporary urban West. This assertion, however, may seem particularly audacious to readers in British Columbia and Manitoba, who are intuitively the most likely to challenge an over-arching regional identity. What we need, therefore, is empirical evidence for this continuity, evidence that convinces our reader before she finishes her coffee or beer that she is indeed living in an attitudinal world anchored by the region's past. Such evidence can be found in public opinion surveys.

Tracking Western Alienation

If we are to assert that western alienation has been an ongoing and central component of the regional political culture of western Canada, then we need some way to track its ebbs and flows over time. Were western Canadians of the 1990s "more alienated" than those of the 1970s, or those of the 1930s? How do contemporary levels of alienation compare to those of the past? Are things getting better or worse? Answering such questions, tracking western alienation over the long haul, is not a straightforward task. Although one can get a sense of alienation through a scan of newspaper editorials and high profile speeches going back over 100 years or more, the views expressed in these forums are not necessarily representative of the public at large. Since the late 1960s, however, western alienation has been brought under the light of public opinion research, with survey questions tapping into feelings of dissatisfaction with federalism and with the region's treatment by the national government and within the national community. The empirical evidence that has accumulated over recent decades enables us to paint a detailed picture of the contemporary western alienation landscape.

These public opinion surveys began, perhaps not coincidentally, in the early years of the Trudeau era, a time when the phrase "western alienation" also began to come into vogue in journalistic commentary and academic research. Three studies in particular established the empirical base and set many of the measurement parameters that would govern public opinion research to this day.

1. In 1969, David Elton conducted the first Alberta survey research into regional discontent.[2] At that time, approximately 55 to 60 per cent of Albertans felt the activities of their national government were discriminatory in at least two ways: (1) the national government tended to respond to the problems and concerns of central Canada and to neglect the West; (2) the policies of the national government were developed to benefit central Canada, often at the

expense of westerners. Among the Alberta respondents, 61 per cent agreed with the statement that "The West usually gets ignored in national politics because the political parties depend upon Quebec and Ontario for most of their votes."

2. In 1971, Richard E. Baird and Thelma Oliver surveyed 906 Alberta respondents within months of the provincial election that brought Premier Peter Lougheed to power. They found 43 per cent of their respondents agreed that "The government in Ottawa is run by Toronto- and Montreal-based people who don't care about the rest of Canada" (a curiously worded question), 53 per cent agreed that "Easterners think we are just a bunch of hicks out here," and 61 per cent agreed that "Western Canadians have to unite behind one party to get anything out of Ottawa,"[3] an early hint of Reform and Canadian Alliance.

3. In 1974, a survey of 221 Calgarians conducted by Roger Gibbins found 72 per cent agreed with the statement that "The economic policies of the federal government seem to help Quebec and Ontario at the expense of Western Canada"; 75 per cent agreed that "Because the political parties depend upon Quebec and Ontario for most of their votes, the West usually gets ignored in federal policies"; and 71 per cent agreed that "It often seems that Western politicians are not taken seriously in the East."[4]

It is important to note that all three of these pioneering studies were conducted in Alberta alone, and one in Calgary alone. They did not include the entire West. The limited nature of the research stemmed from very mundane considerations: in no case was funding available for empirical research across the region, and in any event the researchers were all Alberta-based with a particular interest in the rapidly evolving character of their own province. Nevertheless, the Alberta-centric findings of the early research contributed to an empirical and conceptual conflation of Alberta and the West, in which Alberta data were used as evidence for the *regional* political culture. This in turn set off a good deal of controversy as to whether the alienation landscape in Alberta reflected the regional landscape. Were Albertans truly representative of western Canadians at large? As we will see shortly, it now appears that Alberta was more in step with the region as a whole than it was earlier believed to be. Since these first surveys, a number of public opinion studies conducted across western Canada have demonstrated that feelings of discontent are prevalent throughout the four western provinces. Alberta is by no means a systematic outlier, although there are some issues — such as the NEP and the Kyoto Accord - - that can drive Albertans apart from the regional pattern.

Although survey questions often vary across researchers and across the years due to changing political circumstances, thereby making exact tracking of variations in alienation difficult, it is clear that feelings of discontent have been fairly constant in western Canada over the past three decades. For example, a survey question first used in Calgary in 1974 (see above) was run in regional surveys conducted in 1980 and 1990. It asked respondents if they agreed or disagreed that "The West usually gets ignored in national politics because the political parties depend upon Quebec and Ontario for most of their votes." In a May 1980 poll, conducted shortly after the defeat of the Joe Clark government and the election of a Liberal government virtually devoid of western Canadian representation (the Liberals elected only two MPs in the West), 71 per cent of western Canadians agreed with this statement. By October of that same year, just after the imposition of the National Energy Program, the proportion agreeing jumped to 85 per cent. When asked in a 1990 poll, a full decade later and under very different political circumstances — the Mulroney Conservatives were in power, and the country had just come through the protracted debate over the Meech Lake Accord — the same statement received 86 per cent agreement. Two conclusions are evident: levels of western alienation are responsive to changes in the political environment, but variability begins from a very high base.

Similar sentiments of alienation and unfair treatment are seen in responses to a 1991 survey question that asked respondents if they agreed

FIGURE 3.1:   BELIEF THAT THE WEST IS IGNORED IN
NATIONAL POLITICS

Percentage agreeing with the statement:
"The West usually gets ignored in national politics because the political
parties depend upon Quebec and Ontario for most of their votes."

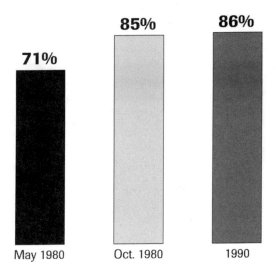

Sources: Canadian West Foundation 1980 (June),
1980 (November); Environics

or disagreed that "My province doesn't get its fair share from Confederation." In all four western provinces, agreement with this statement was much higher than it was for Canada as a whole — almost seven in ten respondents in British Columbia, and in Saskatchewan and Manitoba combined, agreed. Interestingly, and despite Alberta's reputation for being the "hotbed" of western alienation, Alberta respondents were the least alienated, with six in ten agreeing. Somewhat surprisingly, this more moderate response within Alberta came at the time when the Reform Party was building its Alberta bridgehead for the 1993 federal election. It should also be noted from Figure 3.2 that Canadians outside the West are far from immune from the belief that their province is treated unfairly. To the likely astonishment of western Canadians, this belief permeates Quebec and the Atlantic provinces and even pops up in Ontario!

FIGURE 3.2:   PERCEPTIONS OF FAIR SHARE

Percentage agreeing with the statement:
"My province doesn't get its fair share from Confederation."

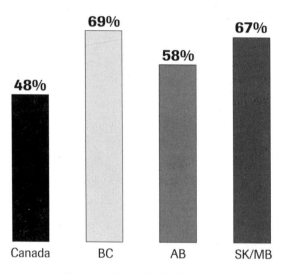

Source: Angus Reid Group

    Public opinion polling provides further evidence that western
Canadian attitudes do respond to changes in the political environment,
although the variability falls within a fairly narrow range. When western Canadian respondents to a 1983 survey were asked how well their
province was represented in Ottawa, only 5 per cent responded that
they were very well represented and 33 per cent felt they were
adequately represented; six in ten responded that they were either
poorly or very poorly represented.[5] At this time the Liberals were in
power, and Liberal MPs from the West were as scarce as the proverbial
hen's teeth. In a September 1984 survey, conducted weeks after the
Mulroney Progressive Conservative landslide brought a slew of western MPs into the federal cabinet and caucus of the governing party,
these figures changed to 12 per cent who thought they were very well
represented and 38 per cent who responded that they were adequately

represented in Ottawa.[6] The interesting thing is not that the Mulroney victory brought a change in public opinion, but rather that the change was so modest. Despite the dramatic change in the regional composition of the national government, those who felt their province was very well or at least adequately represented in Ottawa increased only from 38 to 50 per cent. The facts of the case suggest that the West was indeed well represented within the Mulroney government, but public opinion provides a pale reflection of this. The public's skepticism may well have reflected the deeper reality, and the deeper regional experience, that adequate regional representation does not rest on numbers alone.

Although levels of western alienation have waxed and waned over the years, there is a general consensus that one of the high watermarks was reached in the wake of the fall 2000 federal election. (Another clearly came after the 1993 election, which regionalized the House of Commons and pitted the western-based Reform Party of Canada against the Liberal government.) In the 2000 election, the Liberals won a third consecutive majority government despite thin electoral support in the West (14 seats across the four provinces), and the western-based Canadian Alliance (formerly the Reform Party) increased its seat count in the West without achieving an anticipated breakthrough in Ontario. The election campaign itself had exacerbated regional conflict, and Canadians were left once again with a regionally polarized party system and House of Commons. Not surprisingly, media commentators reported that western Canadians were very dissatisfied with their status within the Canadian federation and felt under-appreciated within Canada. These sentiments were emphatically reflected in the 2001 Canada West Foundation survey,[7] which probed western alienation along three dimensions:

1. **Influence**. Seven in ten western Canadians stated their province does not have its fair share of influence on important national decisions. As Figure 3.3 shows, there were unusually strong provincial differences on this question: over three in four respondents in British Columbia and Saskatchewan agreed that their

province has less than its fair share of influence on important
national decisions, compared to approximately six in ten in both
Alberta and Manitoba. It is noteworthy that four in ten Manitoba
respondents (40.7 per cent) felt their province has about its fair
share of influence on the national stage, making Manitoba the least
"alienated" province on this dimension.

FIGURE 3.3:   INFLUENCE ON IMPORTANT NATIONAL
DECISIONS

Percentage of respondents who stated that their province has
less than its fair share of influence on important national decisions.

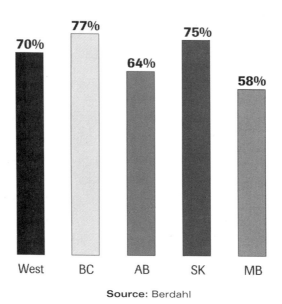

Source: Berdahl

2. **Respect.** Almost two-thirds of western Canadians felt their
    province was not treated with the respect it deserves in Canada.
    The respect question taps strongly into feelings of alienation, and
    the provincial differences in Figure 3.4 are striking. Alberta fell well
    behind Saskatchewan and British Columbia on this measure: in
    Saskatchewan, nearly three-quarters of the respondents reported a

lack of respect for Saskatchewan, while in British Columbia over two-thirds held the same opinion for their own province. Manitoba is also unique on this measure: half of Manitoba respondents felt that their province was treated with the appropriate respect, while half did not. Figure 3.4 illustrates the problems that can occur when national surveys lump together Saskatchewan and Manitoba respondents, and sometimes Alberta respondents, into a common "prairie respondent" category. It is not unusual; in our experience, Saskatchewan and Manitoba are attitudinally the least similar rather than the most similar western provinces.

FIGURE 3.4:   PROVINCIAL RESPECT

Percentage of respondents who stated that their province is not treated with the respect it deserves in Canada.

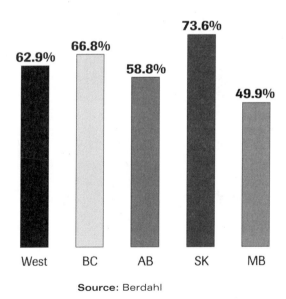

Source: Berdahl

3. **Fair Share.** Six out of ten western Canadians stated their province receives less than its fair share of federal spending on programs and transfers to provincial governments, while nearly four out of

ten (38.6 per cent) felt their province receives about its fair share. (Less than 2 per cent felt that their province receives more than its fair share!) Here again, British Columbia and Saskatchewan stand out as being the most alienated, with Manitoba the least alienated. Indeed, less than a majority of Manitoba respondents felt their province was not receiving its fair share. While it would be an exaggeration to describe Manitobans as content with their federal lot, they are certainly more content than their compatriots elsewhere in the West.

Figure 3.5 FAIR SHARE OF FEDERAL SPENDING

Percentage of respondents stating "less than its fair share" when asked: "Thinking of all the money the federal government spends on different programs and transfers to the provinces, do you think your province receives more than its fair share, less than its fair share, or about its fair share?"

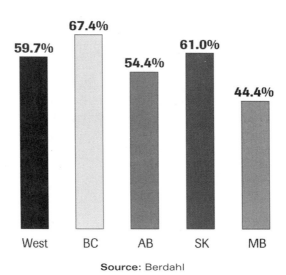

Source: Berdahl

Taken together, the Canada West survey data confirm that feelings of western alienation were as alive and well in 2001 as they were in the 1970s, 1980s, and 1990s. Decades of public opinion research demonstrate that at least during periods in which polling was done, which tend to be periods when regional relationships are frayed, western Canadians have strong and pervasive feelings of discontent with the federal system. They typically feel that both the West and their individual provinces are neglected and underappreciated in the federal system and that regional interests are not appropriately represented or protected. At the same time, there are often significant variations among the four western provinces, albeit variations that do not square with common stereotypes of alienated Albertans and more nationally oriented Saskatchewan residents. In the 2001 Canada West survey, the most alienated respondents were found in British Columbia and Saskatchewan, not in Alberta. At the same time, and consistently, the least alienated respondents tend to be found in Manitoba, reflecting perhaps that province's historic position as the bridge between Ontario and the rest of the West.

Who Is Alienated?

Over the years, in both popular discourse and political rhetoric, attempts have been made to "explain away" regional discontent by linking it to specific demographic groups within the region. For example, as noted above, western alienation is frequently (and incorrectly) seen as an Alberta complaint, shared only to a minor degree by the supposedly more complacent residents of British Columbia, Saskatchewan, and Manitoba. Others argue that western alienation is really rural alienation, that it is not characteristic of the new urban West. By implication, then, western alienation will wane as the West continues to urbanize, a decline that has not been evident over the past 40 years. Still others argue that attitudinal differences are more partisan than regional, that alienated westerners are little more than sore losers in national elections. In addition, it is suggested that disenchanted western voices are primarily male, middle-aged and/or higher income. Western alienation, therefore, is portrayed as a "guy thing" or, more insidiously, as a "white guy thing," out of touch with the politically correct times in which we now live. However, the Canada West Foundation's survey data point to a western reality that is much more complex and nuanced than such quick explanations allow.

1. There is a partisanship gap with respect to western alienation, but respondents identifying with all major parties report high levels of alienation. There is no denying that partisanship shapes attitudes about the West and, more importantly, about the position of the West within the Canadian federal state. Indeed, it would be amazing if Canadian Alliance supporters saw the political world in the same way as do federal Liberals in the West, and they are in fact the most alienated just as Liberal voters are the least alienated. However, many of these partisan differences are ones of degree rather than kind. If we look at the three alienation questions in the 2001 Canada West Foundation survey discussed above, a majority of the supporters for all four official federal parties (Canadian Alliance, Liberal, New Democratic Party (NDP), and Progressive Conservative)[8] report that their province does not get the respect it deserves in Canada, that it does not get its fair share of federal spending and transfers, and that it does not have its fair share of influence on important national decisions. Figure 3.6 illustrates the patterns of both partisan difference and pervasive discontent. While there is no denying that partisanship does play a role (i.e., those identifying with opposition parties are the most alienated), to dismiss western alienation as simply the whining of partisan losers would be incorrect. It is striking that even among federal voters who support parties other than the Canadian Alliance there are strong sentiments of alienation. Partisanship (as identified by federal voting) is part of the picture, but does not tell the complete story.

2. Western alienation is not a "rural issue": both urban and rural residents in western Canada report high levels of alienation. Respondents to the Canada West survey were divided for analysis into three categories: rural (those living in areas with populations

FIGURE 3.6:   PARTISANSHIP AND RESPECT

Percentage of respondents who stated that their province
is not treated with the respect it deserves in Canada.

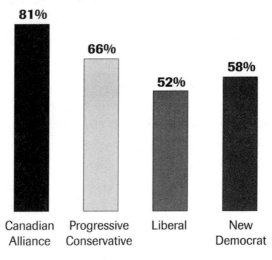

Source: Berdahl

less than 10,000), small urban (those living in urban areas with
populations of 10,000 to 99,999), and large urban (those living in
Census Metropolitan Areas with populations greater than
100,000).[9] Is western alienation largely a rural issue? Based on the
survey, the answer appears to be no. On the respect and influence
questions, there were no statistically significant differences
between urban and rural respondents. Answers to only one of the
three basic alienation questions discussed above showed significant
differences, and the gap between the urban and rural respondents
was not particularly large. Six in ten (60.9 per cent) rural respondents, compared to 54.4 per cent of small urban and 54.9 per cent
of large urban respondents, felt that their province does not
receive its fair share of federal spending and transfers. Thus, the
survey data suggest that alienation is a *western Canadian* issue,
regardless of place of residence within the West. To write western

alienation off as rural alienation is to misunderstand or misrepresent the nature of the phenomenon.

3. There is a generational gap with respect to western alienation, but young people still report high levels of alienation. In fact, there are a number of clear differences among three broad age categories in the West: young (aged 18-34), middle (aged 35-64) and older (aged 65 and over). On most public opinion questions, statistically significant differences are found among these age categories, and this pattern holds for questions of western alienation: compared to middle-aged and older respondents, young respondents do report lower levels of alienation. However, it should be stressed that a majority of 18-34 year olds in western Canada still feel that their province does not get enough respect (54.1 per cent), does not get its fair share of transfers (52.0 per cent), and does not have its fair share of influence (63.1 per cent) on important national decisions. As with partisanship, age is a factor, but a majority of respondents in all age categories report feelings of alienation. To say that the younger generation is *less* alienated is quite different from saying that it is *not* alienated. Again, the difference is one of degree rather than kind. What we don't know is whether the age difference is a generational or life-cycle effect. Will the *relatively* content young respondents maintain their level of alienation as they age, thus injecting a permanent change into the regional political culture, or will they become more alienated as they age, thereby replacing the older cohorts? The question is an important one, but the answer is by no means clear.

4. Alienation is not a gender issue. Women and men do not differ on their responses to any of the three alienation questions included in the CWF survey. Western alienation is not a "guy thing."

So, who are the *most* alienated? Those most likely to report "alienated" responses are older respondents; retirees; middle-income respondents; Canadian Alliance voters; respondents with a grade 12, trade school/college certificate, or incomplete university education; and Saskatchewan and British Columbia respondents. The strongest indicators of alienation are federal voting preference (Canadian Alliance voters) and province of residence (Saskatchewan and British Columbia residents). That said, it must be stressed again that western alienation is common, indeed characteristic, across all age groups, all provinces, all parties, and all communities from metropolitan centres to the rural countryside. Western alienation cannot be explained away by attributing it to one "group." It truly is a regional phenomenon and, therefore, must be understood on regional rather than socio-demographic or partisan grounds.

It is the pervasive nature of western alienation that allows us to speak of a regional political culture into which virtually everyone buys to a degree. It is in turn this regional political culture that enables us to use phrases such as *"western Canadians believe"* or *"the West feels excluded from national decision-making."* If socio-economic, provincial, and partisan differences within the region were more pronounced, such sweeping statements would need constant qualification. In most respects, however, there is no need.

The absence of strong socio-demographic correlates points to another important conclusion. As researchers from the early 1970s on have argued,[10] western alienation is quite distinct from political alienation more generally conceived. The conventional ranks of the politically alienated are those most marginalized from the societal mainstream — the poor, ethnic and racial minorities, and those lacking in education and social skills. The conventional manifestation of alienation is withdrawal from the political process (and other forms of social activity), withdrawal manifested particularly in low rates of electoral and other forms of political participation. Western alienation, however, displays none of these characteristics except for *territorial* marginalization. The ranks of the alienated in western Canada are not filled from the margins of the regional society, and western alienation is not characterized by withdrawal from the political process. To the contrary, and from the earlier agrarian protest parties to Reform and Canadian Alliance, it has been characterized by active political engagement. Political elites in the West, frustrated in their *national* aspirations, have consistently channeled that frustration into constructive efforts to reform the political system. Protest, not apathy, has been the outstanding characteristics of western alienation.

Western Alienation and Separatism

The pervasive and persistent reality of western alienation inevitably leads to concerns about western separatism, particularly when regional discontent in the West is compared to nationalist discontent in Quebec. Is western alienation potentially the same as support for western separatism?[11] Is the former a stepping-stone to the latter? Is support for western separatism an extreme form of western alienation? While there is no denying some degree of correlation — those who believe western Canada would be better off on its own are, by and large, highly disgruntled with Canadian federalism — many western Canadians express feelings of discontent while at the same time adamantly opposing separatist options. Those who support separatism are little more than a small fringe within the vastly larger alienated mainstream, which remains committed to a democratic reform project, despite a frustrating lack of progress.

In the 1971 Alberta study reported above, 12 per cent of the respondents agreed that "Western Canada should have its own separate government, independent of everyone else."[12] This is a surprisingly high percentage given that federal-provincial relations were relatively calm at the time and that the preceding Alberta provincial election, won by the Lougheed Conservatives, had provided very little venting of regional discontent. In the 1974 Gibbins survey also cited above, only 8 of 221 respondents manifested even the most hesitant or conditional support for western separatism.[13] A 1977 Goldfarb study of 544 western Canadian respondents found that 18 per cent in Manitoba, 14 per cent in Alberta, 12 per cent in British Columbia, and 11 per cent in

Saskatchewan agreed that their own province would be better off on its own, separate from Canada.[14]

More comprehensive regional data come from a series of tracking surveys between 1979 and 1981, when emotions in the West ran high due to national election results and the controversial National Energy Program. Western Canadian respondents were asked a hard-line question: "Would you prefer that the provinces of Western Canada become an independent country, join the United States as separate states, or remain part of Canada?" As Figure 3.7 shows, support for an independent West varied somewhat over the two-year period, but at no time did it exceed 8 per cent for the region as a whole. At its peak in November 1980, 13 per cent of Alberta respondents and 7 per cent of British Columbia, Saskatchewan, and Manitoba respondents favoured separation.

FIGURE 3.7:   SUPPORT FOR WESTERN SEPARATISM, 1979–1981

Percentage of respondents who would prefer that western Canada become an independent country.

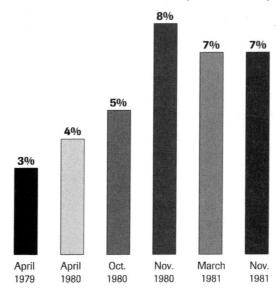

Source: Canada West Foundation

However, while western Canadians may not support a hard-line stance on independence, softer questions on separatism receive considerably higher levels of agreement. For example, the statement, "Western Canadians get so few benefits from being part of Canada that they might as well go it on their own," received agreement from 36 per cent of western Canadians in a 1981 poll and 39 per cent in a 1990 poll.[15] Expressions of separatism, therefore, appear to be an extremely disgruntled expression of western alienation rather than a true desire for an independent West. This is in line with the argument made in Chapter 2 that western alienation can best be seen as frustrated Canadian nationalism rather than as a precursor to support for independence. Nonetheless, it is worth asking how far that frustration can be pushed before it morphs into something more akin to support for independence.

Regional surveys conducted for the Canada West Foundation in 1980 and 1981, years spanning relatively intense dissatisfaction stemming from the 1980 federal election and the NEP, put some useful empirical flesh on the conceptual skeleton of western alienation. As Table 3.1 illustrates, western Canadians are likely to see separation as possible, and a substantial number believe that the West might be better off on its own. At the same time, however, the proportion who would support the formation of an independent West or who, for that matter, would support the West joining the United States as either one or four states was very small even during a period of intense regional discontent.

Polling research suggests that one reason western Canadians do not entertain separatist options is that the vast majority do not believe their economic interests would be advanced. In the 2001 Canada West survey, respondents were asked to agree or disagree with the statement, "My province would be better off economically if it separated from Canada." While levels of disagreement vary, in all four provinces a strong majority disagrees with this idea. On this question, as Figure 3.8 illustrates, the differences between the provinces are strong. Manitoba and Saskatchewan respondents have the highest levels of disagreement, while in Alberta and British Columbia a full quarter of respondents

TABLE 3.1:   ATTITUDINAL SUPPORT FOR WESTERN
              SEPARATISM

	MAY 1980	OCT 1980	MAR 1981	NOV. 1981
% agreeing that "The Western provinces have sufficient resources and industry to survive without the rest of Canada."	53	60	61	59
% agreeing that "Western Canadians get so few benefits from being part of Canada that they might as well go it on their own."	N/A	28	36	32
Would you prefer that the four provinces of western Canada:				
Combine to form one region separate from Canada	4	5	7	N/A
Join the United States	4	3	3	N/A
Remain the same	88	90	87	N/A

Sources: Canada West Foundation 1980 (June);
1980 (November); 1982 (April).

agrees that their province would be better off economically. Given that this question looks at economic interests alone, and does not tap into the social and emotional ties linking respondents to Canada, it is not surprising that alienation has yet to spin into widespread support for separatism. To admit that one's province would be better off economically is still a very big step from arguing that one's province *should* separate from Canada.

Some insight into this distinction can be provided by the ongoing national debate about the possibility of economic and political union with the United States. The empirical evidence certainly suggests that individual Canadians would be better off if Canada were to join the United States, for on many economic measures Americans consistently score higher than do their Canadian counterparts. This reality, however, has not sparked any mass support for greater continental integration.

FIGURE 3.8:   FINANCIAL REWARDS OF SEPARATION

Percentage of respondents who agree with the statement, "My province would be better off economically if it separated from Canada."

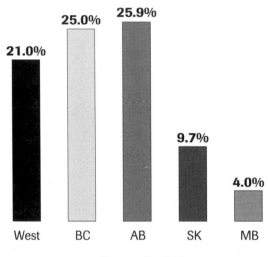

Source: Berdahl

On balance, Canadians seem to believe that it is worth paying an economic price for national independence, and they opt for remaining independent from the United States despite the potential economic gains of union. In a similar fashion, western Canadians who believe that they would be better off as an independent country do not necessarily support an independent West as a consequence. Their first preference is unquestionably a better, more equitable deal within Canada.

There is, of course, a frustrating irony to this situation, one that is often picked up in regional debates. The fact that the vast majority of western Canadians do not support separatism despite high levels of alienation *reduces* the political risks to the national government of ignoring western discontent. Discontent with the status quo in Quebec drives the national political process because it is backed by credible support for a separatist option. Discontent with the status quo in the West fails to drive the political process because it is not backed by credible support for separatism. It can be ignored at little risk.

If we look ahead, the question that must be raised is whether future political and/or constitutional crises might provoke levels of potential support for separatism analogous to what we found with the NEP in the early 1980s. In this context, it is useful to consider the impact of the Kyoto Accord ratification debate on public opinion within Alberta. A survey of 1,000 Albertans conducted between October 20 and 25, 2002, asked respondents if they agreed or disagreed with the following statement: "If Canada ratifies the Kyoto Protocol, Alberta should consider separating from Canada."[16] In Calgary, 23 per cent agreed with the statement, compared to 21 per cent in rural Alberta and 16 per cent in Edmonton. Note, however, that the question still presents a soft option: "Alberta should *consider* separating" rather than "Alberta *should* separate."

Western Alienation in a National Context

As Chapter 1 noted, alienated western Canadians do not exist alone in a sea of national contentment and harmony. Canada is a country of regions and, increasingly, a country of discontented regions. The national and international communities alike are familiar with nationalist/anti-federalist discontent in Quebec, discontent that has come close more than once to breaking Canada apart. Canadians are also becoming more aware of regional discontent emerging from Atlantic Canada. While the sources and expressions of regional discontent vary greatly among western Canada, Quebec, and Atlantic Canada, it is striking that so many Canadians are unhappy with the federal status quo. Western Canadians do not have a monopoly on discontent.

While a complete overview of national public opinion is beyond the scope of this discussion, the following survey data are telling:

1. In a 1991 survey (Figure 3.13), six of ten respondents in every region except Ontario agreed that their province does not receive

its fair share from Confederation. Ontario respondents, on the other hand, were very content with the federal system's treatment of their province. ("And so they should be!" would be the western Canadian response.)

FIGURE 3.9: NATIONAL PERCEPTIONS OF CONFEDERATION'S FAIRNESS (1991)

Percentage of respondents who agree with the statement, "My province doesn't get its fair share from Confederation."

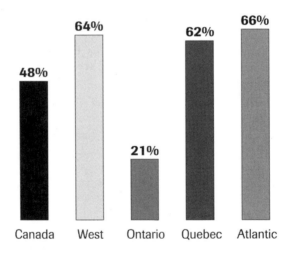

Source: Angus Reid Group

2. A national public opinion survey conducted in 2000 (Figure 3.10) found that although western Canadians were less likely than were other Canadians to agree that "The federal government generally treats all Canadians fairly," respondents in other regions also reported generally high levels of dissatisfaction with Canadian government and federalism.[17]

3. Tracking studies between 1998 and 2001 indicate that while Ontario respondents continue to report high satisfaction with

FIGURE 3.10: NATIONAL PERCEPTIONS OF FAIR TREATMENT
BY THE FEDERAL GOVERNMENT, 1991

Percentage of respondents who agree with the statement,
"The federal government generally treats all Canadians fairly."

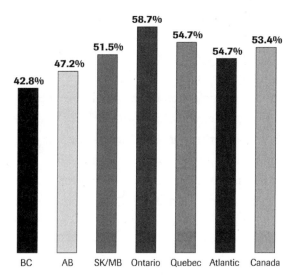

Source: Howe and Northrup

federalism, and while Quebec respondents "are viewing the prac-
tice of federalism more favourably," attitudes in Atlantic Canada
and the West are deteriorating over time. The deterioration in
western Canadian attitudes has been particularly sharp.[18]

Thus, while western Canadians stand apart from other Canadians in
their level of discontent, the difference is not huge. If we take the relatively content residents of Ontario out of the picture, there is little to
distinguish among survey respondents in Atlantic Canada, Quebec, and
the West when it comes to satisfaction with the national government
or the federal system. This raises an important question. If a majority
of all Canadians living outside Ontario is dissatisfied with Canadian
federalism, is it appropriate to look specifically at western alienation?
Or would a more appropriate response be to address the larger, over-

arching issue (or issues) that creates a system in which residents from nine out of ten provinces are unhappy? After all, decades of dealing exclusively with discontent in one region — Quebec — has resulted in a country with greater rather than less regional discontent. Maybe we need to think nationally to address regional discontent.

These are fair questions, and the ideal strategy would be one that looks at both western alienation and the larger challenges facing Canadian federalism. Dealing with western alienation to the exclusion of Atlantic or Quebec concerns would be as foolhardy as past (and ongoing) strategies of dealing with Quebec to the exclusion of other regions. In this sense, regional discontent is like Canada's own game of "whack a mole": once one node of regional discontent seems to disappear, another quickly emerges. Thus an examination of the systemic challenges is clearly in order. However, that examination will take a considerable amount of time — time that may turn into delay or inaction. For this reason, it is necessary that Canadians look more immediately at the western alienation issue. Western alienation continues to grow ever sharper and presents a more immediate challenge to Canadian federalism than does Atlantic discontent or even, arguably, Quebec nationalism; it is a more immediate challenge in part because of the federal government's reluctance to address it. Also, as noted earlier, western alienation is not simply a partisan or policy issue; it embraces larger issues of regional identity and, as such, will require concerted effort if it is to be addressed effectively. This effort will be the subject of the following chapters.

Conclusions

Both the historical analysis in Chapter 2 and the more contemporary public opinion data explored in this chapter have shown that western alienation is a major and enduring component of the regional political culture. The question, then, is how best to deal with western alienation in a way that has permanent effects, that goes beyond partisan alterations in the national government and minor adjustments to public policies. What, in short, are the strategic options for dealing with western alienation? It is to this question that we now turn.

Notes

1   J.A. Archer, "The Prairie Perspective," *One Country or Two?*, ed. R.M. Burns (Montreal, QC: McGill-Queen's University Press, 1971) 247.

2   David K. Elton, "Electoral Perceptions of Federalism: A Descriptive Analysis of the Alberta Electorate," diss., University of Alberta, 1973.

3   The best analysis of this survey is found in Robert R. Gilsdorf, "Western Alienation, Political Alienation, and the Federal System: Subjective Perceptions," *Society and Politics in Alberta: Research Papers*, ed. Carlo Caldarola (Toronto, ON: Methuen, 1979) 168-92.

4   Roger Gibbins, "Models of Nationalism: A Case Study of Political Ideologies in the Canadian West," *Canadian Journal of Political Science*, 10:2 (June 1977): 341-73.

5   Canada West Foundation, *Public Opinion Update, Report No. 17, December 1983* (Calgary, AB: Canada West Foundation, 1983).

6   Canada West Foundation, *Public Opinion Update, Report No. 18, December 1984* (Calgary, AB: Canada West Foundation, 1984).

7   For a full analysis of this survey, see Berdahl, *Looking West*. Some text used in this section is excerpted from this report, with the permission of the author and the Canada West Foundation.

8   Partisanship was measured by the respondent's reported vote in the 2000 federal election, which had taken place only three months before the CWF survey went into the field.

9   The population distinctions are based on Statistics Canada classifications for census data. Respondents were divided in the urban-rural categories based on self-identified postal codes (first three digits).

10   For a detailed discussion of this point, see Roger Gibbins, "Western Alienation and the Alberta Political Culture," Caldarola 143-67.

11   The scholarly literature on western separatism is not large. For what is by far the best of the field, see Larry Pratt and Garth Stevenson, eds., *Western Separatism: The Myths, Realities and Dangers* (Edmonton, AB: Hurtig Publishers 1981).

12   Gilsdorf, "Western Alienation" 271.

13   Gibbins, "Models of Nationalism" 358.

14   See Goldfarb.

15   Canada West Foundation, 1981; Environics, 1990.

16   *Edmonton Sun* 28 October 2002: A1.

17   Howe, Paul and David Northrup, (2000). "Strengthening Canadian Democracy: The Views of Canadians," *Policy Matters* 1,5 (Montreal, QC: Institute for Research on Public Policy).

18   Centre for Research and Information on Canada (2002). *Portraits of Canada 2001* (Montreal, QC: CRIC).

CHAPTER 4

MOVING BEYOND
WESTERN ALIENATION:
Strategic Options and Alternatives

"The West has been defined as a colonial society seeking equality in Confederation. That equality was sought in order that the
West should be like, not different from the rest of Canada."[1]

—W.L. MORTON, historian

Introduction

The discussion to this point has identified western alienation as an
enduring problem for the national community. The quest for equality
that W.L. Morton identified almost 50 years ago has not been achieved,
and regional discontent has, if anything, intensified rather than abated.
Moreover, the West's growing share of the Canadian population, its
contribution to the economy, and its economic potential all mean that
regional discontent has important *national* effects. While it may be an
exaggeration to say that the survival of the country is at stake if western alienation is not addressed, it would not be an exaggeration to say
that Canada's economic performance is at risk. In short, *western alienation is a national issue that should command the attention of the national
government*. It is also a problem for western Canadians. Alienation
constitutes wasteful friction or drag within the political system, can
complicate how public policy priorities are addressed — witness the

perennial federal-provincial conflict over health policy reform — and reflects a limited opportunity for western Canadians to play upon the national stage. It speaks to the loss of human capital, or at the very least to the diversion of that capital into non-productive directions.

The chronic nature of regional discontent should not make those inside or outside the West resigned or complacent; discontent comes at a cost that neither Canadians as a whole nor western Canadians alone should tolerate in an increasingly competitive global environment. Indeed, changes within that environment drive home the dilemma posed by western alienation. Figure 4.1 shows that interprovincial trade has been declining as a proportion of the regional economy while international trade, primarily with the United States, has increased dramatically.[2] As a result, interprovincial trade is weakening as a source of glue for the national community; the domestic Canadian economy matters less and less for western prosperity. At the same time, globalization is challenging the policy capacity and relevance of national governments everywhere, and continental integration is threatening the survival of a distinctive Canadian culture, economy, and public policy universe. The country is under strain that will only increase in the future.

None of these pressures are unique to western Canada. Figure 4.1 demonstrates, for example, that changes in trade patterns have swept across the country; they are as characteristic, perhaps even more characteristic, of the rest of Canada's evolving position within national, continental, and global economies.[3] In the West, however, the pressures interact with and are potentially exacerbated by western alienation. As Ottawa wrestles with Canada's changing position within the North American and global economies, it may pursue policies on issues such as agricultural marketing boards, airline competition, and climate change that will adversely affect regional interests. Admittedly, the federal government in the future will be more constrained in its capacity to influence the regional economy for good or for ill; freight rates, for instance, are now set by markets, and the terms of the NAFTA probably preclude a repeat of the National Energy Program should it ever

FIGURE 4.1:   REAL INTERPROVINCIAL EXPORTS COMPARED
TO REAL INTERNATIONAL EXPORTS, 1981–2000
(% of GDP)

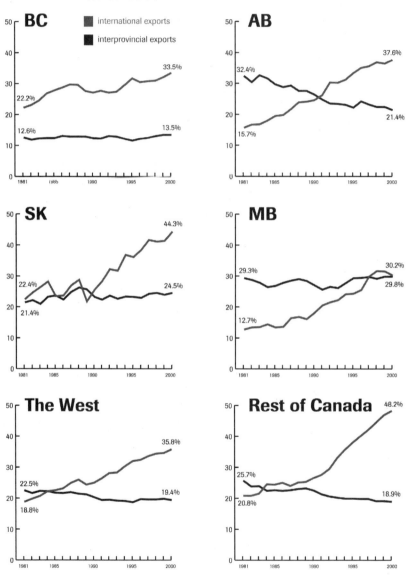

Source: Roach

be contemplated. (The terms of NAFTA do not, however, preclude a climate change strategy that might replicate the effects if not the legislative instruments of the NEP.) Yet, the reduced relevance of the federal government with respect to national and regional economic management has been accompanied by a more assertive federal presence in policy areas that have not been vacated to markets — health care, early childhood development, environmental protection — areas conventionally falling under the legislative jurisdiction of provincial governments. Ottawa is thus both more and less relevant for western Canadians, and this volatile mix has as much potential to enflame as it does to dampen alienation.

REGIONAL POLITICS CAN MAKE FOR STRANGE BEDFELLOWS

During the 1988 federal election campaign, Senator Pat Carney, then Minister of Energy within the Conservative Mulroney government, spoke to a Calgary audience on the merits of the proposed Free Trade Agreement with the United States. She made the argument that Albertans should support the FTA because, once it was in place, Washington would ensure that there would never be another National Energy Program. Thus, a federal minister of the Crown was arguing that western Canadians should look to the United States, a foreign power, for protection from their own national government! Unfortunately, her argument is not without some merit.

However, to identify a problem is not the same as identifying a solution. What, then, can be done to reduce the drag of western alienation on regional and national politics? Our thinking in this respect is framed by a number of assumptions:

1. Regional tensions within the political system reflect more than the immutable facts of geography.

2. To the extent that regional tensions have been exacerbated by public policies and political institutions, they can also be moderated by public policies and institutional reform.

3. At the same time, there is no silver bullet, no single policy or institutional reform that will put western alienation to rest once and for all. Because it is so deeply embedded within the regional political culture, western alienation is relatively impervious to singular acts.

4. In the absence of action, the problems associated with regional discontent are likely to grow rather than diminish as the western economy and population base expand, and as the pressures associated with globalization and continental integration intensify.

Finally, any hope of completely purging regional identities, interests, or even conflicts from the body politic is neither realistic nor desirable. Regional identities contribute to Canada's rich diversity and complexity; thus, to argue that we should outgrow regionalism makes no more sense than to argue that Aboriginal peoples should cease to be Aboriginal, or that the Québecois should abandon a distinct identity.[4] Differing regional interests are inevitable in a country so large and diverse. A more realistic and desirable objective is to reduce regional conflict to the point where it no longer harms the strategic positioning of western Canada within the new global economy and where it does not introduce dysfunctionalities into national political life. Put more positively, *the objective should be a reformed federalism that would increase the opportunities for regional aspirations to be realized.* The ongoing strength of the regional community in the West should be seen as a national asset, not a liability. The goal, therefore, should be national and regional identities that are complementary and mutually reinforcing. In this respect, we have a considerable distance to go.

Given this framework of assumptions, what are the strategic options and alternatives for addressing western alienation? To answer this question we must bring into play at least three sets of actors: the national government, the national party system (and the electoral system upon which it rests), and provincial governments in the West.⁵ We must also recognize two basic strategic directions: engagement or disengagement. By engagement we mean policy and political initiatives explicitly framed to address western aspirations and alienation by greater inclusion of the West into national policy and decision-making. By disengagement we mean initiatives designed to reduce the impact of the national community and government on regional affairs. The discussion that follows looks first at the federal government and discusses a variety of engagement and disengagement issues. It then turns to the national parties and, finally, to provincial governments in the West where the range of options finds its greatest scope and complexity.

The Government of Canada

At first blush, some degree of federal government disengagement from regional affairs might seem inevitable. The dynamics of globalization predict that national governments will become less relevant to citizens over time, since much of their existing policy capacity will be lost to (or embedded within) international agreements such as the WTO and NAFTA, to markets, or to more localized political authorities. The expectation is that powers presently in the hands of national governments will shift up, down, or out to markets, leaving "hollowed out" national governments at the sidelines of major public policy issues. However, while this expectation may capture the general direction of globalization over the long term, it does not reflect the current reality in which national governments still count. It would be difficult to argue, for example, that their role has shrunk in the post-September 11 security environment. If we look more specifically at the conditions for economic prosperity in western Canada, it is clear that the policies and programs of the Government of Canada, for better or for worse, still have considerable bite. It is also the case that what the federal government does *not* do is still important.

Some quick examples can be used to make the general case. First, federal agencies — National Sciences and Engineering Research Council of Canada (NSERC), Social Sciences and Humanities Research Council of Canada (SSHRC), Medical Research Council of Canada (MRC) — are major funders, indeed *the* major funders, of research in postsecondary institutions, and the funding decisions they make in large part determine the national and global competitiveness of these institutions in western Canada. Certainly no one in the postsecondary system is suggesting that federal agencies vacate the field. Second, immigration will become not only an increasingly important determinant of the West's human capital base in the years to come,[6] but will likely remain under the federal government's jurisdiction even though there are opportunities for a more collaborative approach with provincial and even municipal governments. Transportation provides a third example, although here it is the absence of federal policy engagement that is at issue. The transportation infrastructure linking the West to global markets remains as critically important today as it was in the past, but it is an infrastructure that may deteriorate badly if Ottawa continues to absent itself from any significant funding or policy support for the national transportation system. A fourth and obvious example comes from federal tax policy and tax loads. The ability of western firms to compete in global markets, and the capacity of the West to attract and retain human capital, cannot be divorced from the taxation policies of the federal government.

A final example stems from the growing reliance of the regional economy on trade with the United States. As Figure 4.2 illustrates, the importance of north-south trade has increased substantially for all four western provinces, and, therefore, the management of the Canadian-American relationship has also become more important. Management issues extend from the mechanics of border transactions and specific issues such as softwood lumber, fisheries, agricultural subsidies, environmental protection, and pipelines to mega-policy issues such as continental defence and "homeland security." However, this management still lies, and quite likely inevitably lies, primarily in the hands of the federal government even though the costs imposed by disputes may not be borne equally by all regions of Canada. (For example, 50 per cent of Canada's softwood lumber exports to the United States come from British Columbia.)

FIGURE 4.2:   MERCHANDISE EXPORTS TO THE UNITED STATES BY PROVINCE, 1990-2001 (% of total merchandise exports)

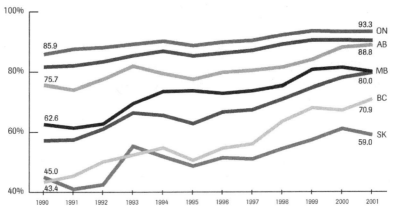

Note: Figures are in current dollars on a customs basis and do not include exports of services.

Source: Roach

There is, then, no doubt as to the real and potential relevancy of federal actions to regional prosperity. Federal disengagement from policy issues driving regional prosperity is impossible unless Ottawa closes its doors. However, a federal role is not enthusiastically embraced by western Canadians because of the deeply-rooted suspicion that federal programs are seldom aligned with regional interests. *This is the core dilemma facing the Government of Canada: federal actions have been seen too often in the past as the problem rather than the cure.* What is needed, therefore, is a *principled foundation* for federal programs and funding decisions. This foundation would be built from the principles of:

- fairness — ensuring that federal spending decisions over time are free from regional bias;

- transparency — ensuring that redistributive federal funding, to the extent that it continues, is explicit and open;
- strategic insight — ensuring that federal programs promote the long-term interests of both the region and the national economy; and
- complementarity — ensuring that federal programs complement those of provincial and urban governments in the West.

If such a foundation could be put into place and sustained, it is possible that western Canadians might support a more positive role for the federal government. However, a more active role *before* regional trust has been restored (or established) could exacerbate rather than moderate alienation.

A PRINCIPLED APPROACH TO IMMIGRATION POLICY

What would a more principled approach to Canadian immigration policy look like? It would ensure that all regions are featured in the international marketing of Canada, that potential immigrants are as aware of the opportunities in Edmonton and Saskatoon as they are of the opportunities in Montreal and Toronto. It would ensure that all provinces receive the same per capita funds for immigrant settlement programs, including language instruction, and that regional quotas are imposed on neither the total number of immigrants admitted nor the funding received. Quebec's entitlement to 25 per cent of new immigrants (a target never met) and 25 per cent of funding (a target that is met) would end. Finally, federal policies would complement and support human capital policies being pursued by provincial governments.

An alternative to a principled foundation would be a political process within which regional interests could be brought to bear in a fashion proportionate to the West's share of the national economy and population. Western Canadians would not be averse to a politicized decision-making process if they were convinced that such a process was not permanently tipped against their interests, in other words, that the political process gave adequate expression to regional interests and aspirations. History, however, tells a rather gloomy story in this respect; hence, the longstanding regional interest in institutional reform, in changing the framework within which and the rules by which the political game is played. Until progress is made on this front — and nobody is holding their breath — it will be difficult to engage the West without some principled foundation being put in place.

At present, confidence in federal programs and funding, and in the national political process, does not exist. Instead, western Canadians tend to believe that federal expenditures, no matter what the program, discriminate against their region. Program revenues are seen to draw disproportionately from western Canadian taxpayers while program benefits flow disproportionately to other regions. As we saw in the last chapter (Figure 3.6), 60 per cent of western Canadians believe that when it comes to the money Ottawa spends on different programs and intergovernmental transfers, their province gets less than its fair share. Figure 4.3 shows that westerners are more likely than other Canadians to believe that their province is singled out for poor treatment by the national government. In effect, federal programs are seen to have, and undoubtedly do have, a redistributive character that works systematically to channel resources outside the West. As a result, it is difficult for residents of the region to believe that national programs will provide net benefits to the West. According to this logic, *the less the federal government does, the better off regional taxpayers will be.* As a consequence, almost no one in the West suggests that the problem of alienation will go away if Ottawa simply throws enough money at it or that the key to regional prosperity is to be found in additional federal spending. To the contrary, the more Ottawa spends, the worse the problem becomes so long as federal spending is redistributive in character. Thus, there is no interest in the "profitable federalism" championed by Quebec leaders such as Robert Bourassa in the 1970s and 1980s, and certainly no expectation that the term would ever apply to the West. Regional fairness and equity in federal programming are sufficiently ambitious goals.

FIGURE 4.3:   WESTERN CANADIANS STAND APART

Percentage of respondents who stated that their province
is treated worse than other provinces by the federal government.

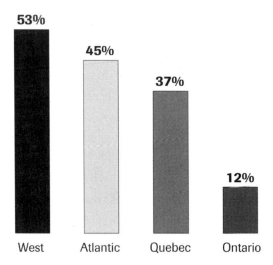

Source: 2000 Canadian Election Study, Blais *et al.*

This wariness of federal programs may help explain the puzzle that regional prosperity is as likely to fan as it is to douse the embers of western alienation. Albertans, for example, are often seen to be at the forefront of the alienated even though Alberta has been one of the most prosperous provinces in recent decades. Alienation, however, is not generated by economic distress, nor is it primarily a call for relief or assistance. It is a call for equity and fairness within federal government programs, a call not restricted to those with relatively low incomes or limited opportunities. As we saw in Chapter 3, there is little or no correlation between individual prosperity, and indeed provincial prosperity, and levels of alienation.

There is, then, little enthusiasm for a western equivalent of the Atlantic Canada Opportunities Agency (ACOA), a federal agency with reasonably deep pockets and the mandate to promote regional economic development and diversification. There is greater support for

Western Economic Diversification Canada (WD), a more modest and lower profile federal agency charged with cost-recovery business loans, advice to small business, and strategic investment. WD also provides the federal government with a strategic policy window on the West and has been the lead agency for federal government engagement with urban policy issues in the region. (The Vancouver Agreement, which tackles drug-related problems in Vancouver's East End, is a current example.) Any substantial expansion of WD's economic development or redistributive role would be viewed with suspicion, although a more powerful voice for WD within the federal bureaucracy would be welcome. On symbolic grounds alone, dismantling WD would be seen as a blow to the West.

ACOA AND WD

The mandate of WD is "to promote the development and diversification of the economy of Western Canada and to advance the interests of the West in national economy policy."[7] ACOA's quite different mandate is both more specific and more general: to promote economic development in Atlantic Canada "in order to increase the number of jobs and earned income of Atlantic Canadians."[8] The explicit job creation mandate for ACOA, as opposed to the diversification mandate of WD, is accompanied by significantly greater financial resources even though the regional population served by ACOA is equivalent to only 25 per cent of the western Canadian population. In the 2002-03 spending estimates, for example, WD's budget was $130,200,000, exclusive of statutory liabilities and the Infrastructure Canada Program, whereas ACOA's budget was $319,400,000, again exclusive of statutory liabilities and the Infrastructure Canada Program. On a per capita basis, WD's budget works out to $14.50 for every resident of western Canada whereas ACOA's budget works out to $139.74 per capita.

It is also clear that western Canadians, like all Canadians, will seek assistance from Ottawa in particular cases. Drought conditions on the Prairies, for example, have led to requests for short-term agricultural assistance, and farmers competing for international markets are seeking federal assistance to offset the large subsidies provided to their competitors in the European Union and United States. In some cases, that assistance may be targeted to the West alone rather than being universal in its application, although this was not the case with the federal government's cost-shared agricultural aid package introduced in the spring of 2002. Over all, however, there is little interest in ongoing programs targeted specifically at the West. The greater concern is for regional fairness and equity in universal programs targeted to all Canadians.

"FARMER PLEADS WITH MARTIN FOR ASSISTANCE"

REGINA — Federal Finance Minister Paul Martin came face to face with the prairie farm crisis on Thursday.

"I'm a 47-year-old farmer, I'm virtually done," Arnie Brickner told Martin after the minister gave a speech [to] the Saskatchewan Association of Rural Municipalities. "My wife has worked off the farm now for two years and I'm her dependent. I don't make enough on the farm. She writes me off on her income tax. That's pretty degrading when you have been paying income tax for many years. It puts a kind of nail in the coffin if you don't want to get out of farming."

Martin appeared dumfounded by Brickner, who was nearly in tears as he told the Finance Minister his story. "You cannot stand in front of a person who's in near tears and in dire straits and not be tremendously touched," the Minister said after the encounter. Martin said the federal government and the provinces were working toward a new deal on farm aid.[9]

If spending more is not an option for Ottawa in addressing either regional frustrations or aspirations, what about spending less? As noted above, there is a prevalent belief that regional economic development would be best served by Ottawa stepping back, getting out of the way, rather than by stepping in. At times, this neo-liberal vision can be seen peeking out from behind the policy platforms of the Reform Party of Canada, in the past, and now the Canadian Alliance. Would it make sense, therefore, to move towards a "nightwatchman" model for the federal government in which it provided only the basics of defence, security, and the rule of law? Regional support over the last decade for Reform/Alliance would suggest that a nightwatchman model would be an effective strategy for wooing the West. If this partisan support primarily reflects ideological enthusiasm for the small government component of the Reform/Alliance platforms, then it might help crack the nut of western alienation. (What it might do for the government's support in other regions is another matter altogether.) Promoting regional prosperity by maximizing the "jingle in the jeans" of taxpayers could have considerable appeal based not only on the intrinsic attractiveness of low taxes but also on the belief that existing tax dollars are not being used fairly or effectively by the federal government.

AIRPORT SECURITY TAX

The Airline Travellers Security Charge, imposed in April 2002, has reinforced western perceptions about the nature of federal programs. First, the tax of $24 on a roundtrip ticket (the similar US tax has a $10 ceiling) will bring in over $430 million in its first year and up to $950 million annually thereafter to fund the Canadian Air Transport Security Agency, which will have estimated annual expenses of only $200 million. Second, the tax will impose a differentially heavy hit on regional airlines and air travel in the West, given that short haul flights face the same ticket tax as do transcontinental and international flights. A return ticket between Calgary and Edmonton, for instance, has the identical tax as a roundtrip ticket between Toronto and Rome. There is, then, a familiar pattern: the taxes collected are far in excess of the costs of providing the service, western Canadian firms (e.g., Westjet) are disproportionately hurt, and western Canadian travellers pay a proportionately higher tax. The goal of greater security is not questioned, but the policy tools chosen to achieve that goal are believed to be unfair. For western Canadian observers, it is further evidence of a general public policy pattern that can be traced back to the National Policy of 1879. In the words of *Vancouver Sun* columnist Barbara Yaffe, "Ottawa finds yet another way to ruin Canadian businesses."[10]

However, historical patterns of partisan support and public expenditures in the West suggest a different conclusion. The CCF and particularly the NDP have been successful in forming provincial governments in Manitoba, Saskatchewan, and British Columbia and certainly have been more successful in the West than in any other region. At the turn of this century, for example, the NDP held power in every western province except Alberta. And, in terms of support for big government, it is not even clear that Alberta is an outlier. When times have been good, Progressive Conservative governments in Alberta have been big spenders; the Peter Lougheed governments, emphatically endorsed by the provincial electorate, routinely led the country in terms of per capita program spending. Some of these trends, it is true, have abated in recent years. Ralph Klein's government in Alberta has been episodically less enthusiastic about big government (although not as opposed as its rhetoric might suggest), and Gordon Campbell's Liberal government in British Columbia is hurtling down a small-government trajectory. Nonetheless, the general conclusion is that western Canadians do not reject government activism per se; it is activism by the federal government that rings alarm bells. Resistance to big government reflects the painful history of western alienation more than it reflects the ideological predispositions of the western Canadian electorate. It is fueled by the inbred conviction that any expansion of the federal government's role is paid for disproportionately by western Canadian taxpayers and that it disproportionately benefits other regions. The electoral appeal of Reform and Canadian Alliance likely has more to do with "the West wants in" than with regional ideological support for small government.

We also have to ask if a nightwatchman role for Ottawa would provide an effective public policy framework for the West. Would it ensure or curtail regional economic prosperity? It can be argued that at the very least the federal government has an important role in strengthening transportation linkages between western producers and global markets, in creating healthy and sustainable urban environments, and in addressing the myriad challenges facing Aboriginal peoples. There

IDEOLOGICAL DISTINCTIVENESS HARD TO DISCERN

The 2000 Canadian Election Study survey of 3,613 respondents found few ideological differences between voters in Ontario and the West. For instance, public policy preferences with respect to homosexual marriages, immigration, and juvenile offenders were virtually identical. While only one-quarter of Ontario respondents supported tax cuts, compared to one-third of the western Canadian respondents, even this difference is very modest.[11] It certainly does not account for the Liberal dominance of Ontario and the Alliance dominance of the West in the 2000 national election.

may also be human capital needs that cannot be addressed fully, quickly, or easily by provincial governments acting alone or together, needs complicated by the scale of interprovincial and international mobility. However, defending a positive role for the federal government requires confidence that Ottawa will carry out its responsibilities and activities in a neutral fashion, and this takes us back to the core of western alienation. The largest obstacle for an activist national government is to be found in the spirit of western alienation rather than in the ideological make-up of the region. Western Canadians will resist a more active federal government as long as they believe that they will pay a disproportionately large share of the cost for expanded federal programs and receive a disproportionately small share of the benefits. Those who believe in active government find it makes more sense to direct this enthusiasm towards provincial policies and programs.

The bottom line for Ottawa is the need to respect federalism, the division of powers, and the integrity of provincial governments. This does not necessarily mean that the federal government should withdraw from such areas as health policy and early childhood development, or that it refrain from engaging in urban affairs. However, it does suggest a more collaborative approach to jurisdictional overlaps, less unilateralism by the Government of Canada on the policy front, greater western Canadian representation within the national political system, and a less abrasive style of national leadership. The manner in which the federal government proceeded with the ratification of the Kyoto Accord suggests that its well of respect for federalism can easily run dry.

In drawing this discussion of the Government of Canada's role to a close, we must also consider disengagement strategies and, more specifically, the option of doing nothing explicit to address either regional discontent or aspirations. It is sometimes believed that western alienation will wane with the passage of time and generational change, that younger western Canadians will slough off the regional fixations and angst of their parents and grandparents. The new generation, in short, may be ready to "move on." Such generational change may — and we stress *may* — be reinforced by the corrosive effect of globalization on national and, by implication, regional identities. If this is the case, then an appropriate strategy for the federal government might simply be to sit tight, to wait for a new generation of western Canadians who will throw in the towel and get on with lives no longer marked by regional discontent and perhaps not even by regional identities. This strategy has some appeal, not the least of which is its low cost and attractiveness to other regional electorates. As past experience has shown, ignoring the West frees up Ottawa's time, attention, and financial resources for other regional interests.

WAITING FOR THE SEPARATISTS TO DIE

The federal government's national unity strategy in Quebec has been informed in part by assumptions about the political effects of demographic change. Given that Quebec nationalism found its most militant expression in the late 1960s and early 1970s, it has been assumed that support for an independent Quebec will gradually wane as the separatist generation ages and eventually dies. It is also assumed that the younger generation moving into political power in the wake of the separatist generation is less committed to the separatist cause, a transformation epitomized by Mario Dumont and his party, the Action Démocratique du Quebec (ADQ). However, the reality of demographic and generational change is more ambiguous. True, younger Québecois seem less committed to the goal of an independent Quebec, but there is no evidence that they are any more attached to Canada than were their separatist forbears. They may share a general cynicism about the national government and political life more broadly with their generational compatriots across Canada and may be less enthusiastic about another referendum on independence, but this says little about how they would vote if a referendum were to be forced upon them. The dream of a sovereign, independent Quebec is unlikely to die with the first generation of Quebec sovereigntists.

The odds are, however, that indifference and inaction constitute a risky and, quite likely, a foolish strategy. Certainly, it has not worked to date even though it has been practiced for generations. Moreover, as we saw in Chapter 3, alienation is not the exclusive preserve of the old and aging; it is not a kind of male menopause writ large upon the political world. Although those aged 18 to 34 report lower levels of alienation than do older survey respondents, their levels are low only in a relative sense. Younger respondents as a group are *less* alienated rather than *un*alienated. Generational change alone will do little to move the yardsticks for western alienation. In this respect, we also know that regional and national political cultures are slow to change. As the "je me souviens" motto on Quebec licence plates illustrates, current perceptions of political reality are anchored by the immutable facts (and mythologies) of history. Finally, it is worth noting how much such a disengagement strategy differs from the active engagement strategy Ottawa has adopted in the battle to win the hearts, minds, and electoral support of "soft" federalists in Quebec (i.e., those uneasy with the federalism status quo but seeking remedies within the Canadian constitution). In this latter case, the federal government for decades has used a combination of aggressive rhetorical engagement, effective political representation, "visibility" campaigns, sponsorship and advertising programs, and massive federal spending to combat the threat posed by sovereigntists in Quebec. Only in the West, it appears, do passivity and indifference have strategic appeal to the federal government.

A do-nothing strategy by Ottawa may feed the apathy and with-drawal from electoral politics that is increasingly characteristic of young Canadians. Young western Canadians, joined in significant numbers by their older compatriots, may simply drift away from the federal government and the national community, just as the federal government is seen as disengaging itself from their concerns and aspirations. A federal government unconnected to the future aspirations of the West becomes a government that is irrelevant at best and an obstacle at worst. It is important, therefore, to promote a national strategy of active engagement with the chronic condition of western alienation. The rudiments of this strategy are clear: fairness and equity in federal programming, greater collaboration with provincial governments, an end to rhetorical assaults on the region during election campaigns, and an explicit recognition of the West's current and potential contribution to national prosperity. This is not rocket science; the only difficult component seems to be mobilizing the political will.

The National Party System

To this point we have discussed the Government of Canada in a rather abstract fashion. At any point in time, however, the national government is animated and driven by the particular party holding a majority or at least a plurality of seats in the House of Commons. It is difficult, therefore, to discuss what the national government *might* or *should* do without also addressing the party system upon which national governments rest. The issue is not how national governments in the abstract might respond strategically to the challenge of western alienation, but rather how Liberal, Alliance, Conservative, or NDP governments might respond. In the present circumstances, our primary interest is in the potential strategic response by Liberal governments.

The partisan history of western Canada offers little hope that the party system, in whole or in its specific parts, will provide a vehicle for addressing either western alienation or regional aspirations. The party system has been more the source of regional discontent than a vehicle through which discontent might be addressed or moderated. Western-based parties — the Progressive Party of Canada, Social Credit, the CCF, the Reform Party of Canada, and the Canadian Alliance — have failed to win national power, and even national influence has been questionable. The Reform Party's clarion call that "the West wants in" was widely derided outside the West as narrow regionalism unsuitable to a truly national party, although "Quebec wants in" has been the informal federalist mantra for generations, and "Ontario is in" is a fact of life. The historical lesson is that western-based parties do not win national office, and national parties explicitly appealing to western regional interests are rare. Indeed, the party system has helped define "regional" in the case of the West, and the West alone, as somehow antithetical to "national." Parties based largely in Ontario and Quebec are self-defined as national, a definition generally accepted by the media and elite political discourse. Parties based largely in the West are defined, and defined successfully by their opponents and the media, as regional. The West is the only Canadian region earmarked in this fashion and the only region with interests assumed to be at odds with the national interest, whatever that might be. But we digress.

WAKE UP, ALBERTA, AND JOIN THE LIBERAL TEAM!

It is sometimes argued that one obvious solution to western alienation has been ignored, particularly by Alberta voters and even more specifically by Calgary voters, and that is to vote Liberal, join the team, and have a seat at the cabinet table. Western alienation from this perspective is seen as the inevitable consequence of failing to support the winning team; it is the expected price to be paid. The alienated are just sore losers in the great political game. It is by no means clear, however, that if the whole country voted Liberal, regional discontent would evaporate. In 1984, virtually the whole country supported Brian Mulroney's Progressive Conservatives, and yet the Reform Party of Canada was born in 1987 and the Bloc Québecois in 1992. Decades of federal Liberal dominance in Quebec have been coupled with successive sovereigntist victories in provincial campaigns, and in Ontario the federal Liberals' hegemony in the late 1990s and early 2000s did not prevent bitter intergovernmental relations with the Mike Harris Conservative governments. The argument that the road to regional tranquillity is paved by votes for the dominant party of the day is too simplistic by far. It is also insulting and undemocratic; fair and equitable government should not be conditional on partisan electoral support. Good government is an entitlement, not a partisan perk.

The basic reality is that political parties with aspirations to form the national government will pitch their party platforms and legislative behaviour to where the bulk of the electorate resides, although here it should be noted that there are now substantially more seats in the West than in Quebec. (Perhaps the law of electoral gravity does not apply in this case.) Political parties, moreover, are private organizations beyond public policy control. To argue that parties should behave in a certain way carries no moral or practical force; parties will do what it is in their best interest to do. At the same time, parties do make strategic choices that can have very substantial regional effects. David Smith, for example, argued persuasively in 1985 that the Liberal weakness in western Canada during the 1970s and early 1980s was not pre-ordained but a matter of strategic choice:

> The provinces today see no defenders of their interests at the center. That is the source of the demand for institutional change: the belief that the central government does not understand the regions, that it does not hear them. On this, however, the regions are wrong. They do not see the real issue. The governing party can court the regions at any time, just as governing parties did in the past. The truth is that the Liberals under Mr. Trudeau chose not to do so, and the reason was that the governing party held a different view of Canada.[12]

Other examples of regional strategizing are not difficult to find. The decision of the Reform Party to reconstitute itself as the Canadian Alliance was driven by the need to escape a regional electoral box, to build a broader national image and appeal. In the 2000 federal election, the Liberal party ran a campaign designed to shove Alliance back into that very box, a campaign that entailed disparaging the Alliance by disparaging the West (and thereby disparaging the West by disparaging the Alliance). It was assumed that if the Alliance could be portrayed as a western-based party, then it would also be seen as a party espousing values unacceptable to the Canadian mainstream. And, admittedly, the Alliance provided ample ammunition in this respect to their partisan opponents.

The strategic choices that parties make are governed by more than the regional distribution of the electorate; they are also shaped by the electoral system within which parties operate. In the Canadian case, the electoral system is one that tends to exaggerate regional divisions and reward partisan appeals based on regional cleavages. This argument was first developed in the late 1960s by Alan Cairns, who demonstrated convincingly that regional cleavages are greater among parties and within the House of Commons than they are within the electorate.[13] In short, Canadian voters are far less regionalized than is their political system. Perhaps the best illustration of this effect came in the 1980 election when the Liberals won only two seats in the West, both in Manitoba, even though they obtained a respectable 23 per cent of the popular vote across the region. As a consequence of this electoral distortion, the West's voice at the federal cabinet table was barely audible and quite likely ignored. The imposition of the National Energy Program eight months after the 1980 election was not a coincidence but rather a direct product of the electoral system and of the regionally distorted parties and national governments produced by that system.

Since that time, electoral distortions have only worsened. As Table 4.1 shows, the federal Liberals captured virtually every Ontario seat in the 1993, 1997, and 2000 elections with just over 50 per cent of the popular vote, therefore giving Ontario MPs a huge presence within the national government. Over the same three elections, first Reform and then the Canadian Alliance picked up a higher proportion of seats in the West than their regional share of the popular vote, but were all but shut out of Ontario despite capturing 20 to 25 per cent of the Ontario popular vote. Table 4.2 shows that although less than 60 per cent of the total Reform/Alliance popular vote came from western Canada, virtually all of their seats came from the West. The fact that over one Reform/Alliance voter in three lived in Ontario found no reflection in the regional distribution of seats. Thus, a national electorate only moderately divided along regional lines, when fed through the electoral system, yielded a regionally fractured and polarized House of Commons. Reform/Alliance seats in the West overshadowed significant electoral support in Ontario, and the Liberals' hegemony in Ontario overshadowed reasonable electoral support for the Liberals in western Canada.

TABLE 4.1:   PERCENTAGE OF THE ONTARIO POPULAR VOTE
AND SEATS WON BY THE LIBERALS, 1993–2000.

	% ONTARIO POPULAR VOTE	% ONTARIO SEATS
1993	52.9%	99.0
1997	49.5	98.1
2000	51.5	97.1

TABLE 4.2:   REFORM/ALLIANCE VOTES AND SEATS FROM
THE WEST AND ONTARIO

	% TOTAL VOTE COMING FROM WEST	% TOTAL SEATS COMING FROM WEST	% TOTAL VOTE COMING FROM ONTARIO	% TOTAL SEATS COMING FROM ONTARIO
1993	57.7%	98.1	38.4	1.9
1997	59.9	100.0	35.3	0.0
2000	57.8	97.0	32.1	3.0

In the ten general elections from 1968 to 2000 inclusive, the Liberals averaged 26.0 per cent of the popular vote across the West but won on average only 15.0 per cent of the seats. In the 1993, 1997, and 2000 elections, Reform/Alliance averaged 43.7 per cent of the popular vote across the West while winning 66.7 per cent of the regional seats in the House of Commons. Thus, the electoral system promotes partisan homogeneity within the West, although its magnitude pales beside the homogenization of Ontario. Compared to the Ontario case, the West reflects a diverse partisan array of federal MPs.

It is not surprising that these regional distortions have sparked a call for electoral reform to bring the regional distribution of seats in the House more into line with the regional distribution of the popular vote. If applied to the 2000 election results, such a reform would yield more Liberal seats in the West, more Alliance seats in Ontario, and quite likely more Progressive Conservative and NDP seats everywhere. Advocates of electoral reform also point out that apart from a few oddities, including the "Senatorial floor" which guarantees at least four House seats for Prince Edward Island, electoral reform can be achieved without constitutional amendment or provincial consent. There is no need to "open up the constitutional can of worms" to address electoral reform.

The quest for electoral reform has been strengthened by a growing perception in the West, particularly in British Columbia, that both the region as a whole and individual provinces are systematically under-represented in the House of Commons. As Table 4.3 shows, this perception is both correct and incorrect. The two fastest growing provinces, British Columbia and Alberta, are under-represented because the distribution of seats in the House inevitably lags changes in the regional composition of the population. However, British Columbia and Alberta shortfalls in this respect are offset by the over-representation of more slowly growing Saskatchewan and Manitoba. On balance, and only slightly, the West receives fewer seats in the House than it is entitled to on the basis of population alone, but the under-representation is concentrated in the western half of the region. If, as proposed following the release of the 2001 Census, Alberta and British Columbia each receive two additional seats, then the West as a whole will have 29.9 per cent of the national population and 29.8 per cent of the seats in the House, although Alberta and British Columbia will still be under-represented.[14]

TABLE 4.3:   REGIONAL AND PROVINCIAL REPRESENTATION
IN THE HOUSE OF COMMONS

	% NATIONAL POPULATION, 2001	% SEATS IN HOUSE OF COMMONS, 2001	% SEATS IN HOUSE OF COMMONS, 2005*
British Columbia	13.0	11.3	11.7
Alberta	9.9	8.6	9.1
Saskatchewan	3.3	4.7	4.5
Manitoba	3.7	4.7	4.5
West	**29.9**	**29.3**	**29.8**

*Based on the proposed addition of two seats each for Alberta and British Columbia and three seats for Ontario.

The distorting effects of the electoral system dampen the West's political voice in the national government. While this is not an automatic effect of the first-past-the-post, single-member constituency electoral system, it has been the practical effect during Liberal governments stretching back at least to the early 1960s. Not surprisingly, therefore, as Figure 4.4 shows, western Canadians tend to be strong supporters in principle of electoral reform. This should not suggest, however, an equally strong political *movement* for reform. In fact, such a movement is extraordinarily tough to mobilize. Incumbent governments, federal or provincial, are the beneficiaries of electoral distortions and thus are never enthusiastic about reform. (Provincial government support for national electoral reform could well boomerang into support for provincial electoral reform.) The political parties have ranged from indifferent support to outright hostility. It is difficult to imagine, for example, that the federal Liberal caucus in Ontario would argue for a more equitable distribution of seats. For its part, the Alliance would pick up seats in Ontario but lose seats in the West. The human problem with all of this is that in any discussion of electoral reform, the potential losers — e.g., up to 50 Liberal MPs from Ontario — are at the table while the potential winners are purely hypothetical, without a human face or supportive colleagues in the room. We should also note that the public policy case for electoral reform is not well-developed; it is not necessarily the case that a House based on a different electoral system would deliver public policies more supportive of regional economic prosperity or of national policy goals.

In the short run, therefore, the national prospects for electoral reform are bleak. At the same time, however, electoral reform is being vigorously pursued by the Liberal government in British Columbia, despite the fact that any reform would erode the Liberals' 78-seat majority in the provincial legislature (the opposition NDP elected only two members). Electoral reform is also on the provincial agenda for Prince Edward Island and makes an episodic appearance in Ontario. There is a chance, then, that provincial initiatives might help drive a national debate on electoral reform.

Should the national case for electoral reform be advanced, it will be tied only in part, perhaps a small part, to western alienation. The stronger case derives from concerns about the representative character of Canadian political institutions and the concentration of political power in the parliamentary system.[15] In the three elections from 1993 to 2000 inclusive, the Liberals averaged 56.1 per cent of the seats in the House of Commons with only 40.2 per cent of the national popular vote. The fact that national governments elected with approximately 40 per cent of the popular vote can govern with no effective checks or balances is more likely to animate reform discussions than are regional distortions. Adding to this debate will be the electoral reform experiences of other western democratic states including Italy, New Zealand, and, shortly, Great Britain. Canada increasingly stands alone, apart from the United States, in its fidelity to an electoral system originally designed for the late eighteenth and early nineteenth centuries.

In the long–run, electoral reform may well deliver some institutional

FIGURE 4.4:   REGIONAL SUPPORT FOR ELECTORAL REFORM

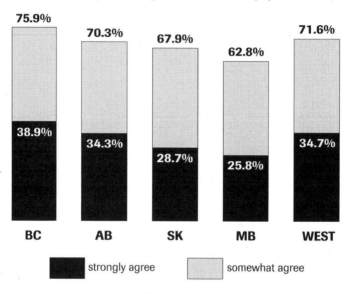

"Do you agree or disagree that Canada should replace
the present electoral system with an electoral system based
on proportionate representation – that is, a system that distributes
seats to each party according to its share of the popular vote?"

Source: Berdahl

relief from regional distortions in the electoral system and from regional discontent. However, the long run may indeed be long, and thus it is important to address potentially shorter-term strategic responses to western alienation. Many of these lie within the reach of provincial governments.

Provincial Governments in the West

Provincial governments face two basic strategic choices in dealing with the multitude of issues embedded in western alienation (as does the federal government). The first option is active engagement, seeking ways in which the West's status and influence within the national community and the status and influence of individual western Canadian provinces can be enhanced. The second is disengagement, seeking ways in which the impact of the national community on the West and on individual western Canadian provinces might be reduced. The first option follows the basic logic of "the West wants in," while the second is more defensive in spirit, at least to the point where political independence is considered. The difference between the federal and provincial governments is that the latter confront this choice day in and day out as they address a policy agenda that is deeply entangled in relationships with the broader national community and its government. Only Ottawa has the unfortunate luxury of being able to ignore western alienation altogether.

A strategy of engagement, of seeking ways to maximize the status and influence of the West in national affairs, is clearly the option we favour. As the analysis to come in subsequent chapters will illustrate, it is an option virtually forced upon the West by the nature of the region's policy agenda and by the intergovernmental context of policy making in an increasingly interdependent world. However, to explore engagement strategies in the depth they deserve, we first have to have a thorough understanding of that policy agenda. This comes in Chapter 5. We also have to understand the intergovernmental environment and how policy challenges are tackled in an interdependent world. This will be addressed in Chapter 6. At this point we want to discuss a number of disengagement strategies. All share a common theme: western alienation could be reduced by lodging more power in the hands of governments western Canadians truly control and less power in a federal government lying beyond the effective influence of western Canadians. More influence within the national government is abandoned as a lost or futile cause; instead, ways are sought to empower provincial and regional communities in the West, to provide in effect more expansive and/or autonomous home rule. The strategic options line up roughly along a continuum running from the status quo to greater disengagement:

- firewall strategies, by which provincial governments would more fully occupy their existing constitutional domain and resist incursions into that domain by the federal government;

- greater decentralization of the constitutional division of powers in order to give provincial governments an expanded legislative domain; and
- variants of an independent West, or parts thereof.

Readers will recognize a basic parallel with the range of options that have been explored by Quebec nationalists over the past 50 if not 100 years — protecting Quebec's existing constitutional domain, expanding that domain, and achieving some form of sovereignty association or independence for Quebec. However, although the range of alternatives is similar, we will see that they play out quite differently in the West and Quebec. It should also be noted that Senate reform is not on our list of disengagement strategies. The variety of Senate reform models all share a common ambition, that is, to enhance the political power of the regions within the federal government. A reformed Senate is the way for the West to get in, to exercise greater influence in the national capital. Senate reform is, therefore, an engagement strategy and as such will be discussed in Chapter 6.

Firewall Strategies

At the present time, provincial governments in western Canada, and for that matter across the board with the possible exception of Quebec, do not fully occupy their existing constitutional "space." There are legislative powers invested in provincial legislatures by the Constitution that they do not exercise. There are also policy fields such as health where the federal government has essentially bought its way into provincial jurisdictions through the use of its spending power and policy fields that provincial governments have vacated in response to federal initiatives. For example, although Quebec has established its own Quebec Provincial Pension plan, no other province has followed suit, even though there is no constitutional barrier to doing so. (There may be public policy constraints relating to effectiveness, efficiency, and equity, but they are another matter.) In short, provincial governments could do more *without any formal modification to the constitutional division of powers.* Greater *de facto* decentralization could occur without *de jure* constitutional change.

In the wake of the 2000 general election, an influential group of Albertans proposed to do just that — to pursue a strategy that would enable the provincial government to occupy more fully its existing constitutional space, thereby walling off a larger portion of the public policy arena from the federal government. In an open letter to Alberta Premier Ralph Klein,[16] the authors of what became known as the Firewall Strategy reacted to the 2000 election campaign, which in their view was designed "to marginalize Alberta and Albertans within Canada's political system."[17] The letter, really a manifesto, went on to state:

> We believe the time has come for Albertans to take greater charge of our own future. This means resuming control of the powers that we possess under the Constitution of Canada but that we have allowed the federal government to exercise. Intelligent use of these powers will help Alberta build a prosperous future despite a misguided and increasingly hostile government in Ottawa.

More specifically, the authors called for withdrawal from the Canada Pension Plan and the creation of an Alberta Pension Plan, for Alberta to collect its own revenue from personal income tax, for the creation of a provincial police force,[18] for the Alberta government to "resume provincial responsibility for health-care policy," and for Senate reform to be brought back onto the national agenda through Section 88 of the Supreme Court's decision in the Quebec Reference case. The authors concluded by saying that "it is imperative to take the initiative, to build firewalls around Alberta, to limit the extent to which an aggressive and hostile federal government can encroach upon legitimate provincial jurisdiction." As one of the authors, Tom Flanagan, stated at the time, "our group's position is not independence or separation, it's an autonomous position."[19]

Throughout the letter, the authors drew parallels with Quebec, arguing that with respect to many of their proposals — a provincial pension plan, a provincial police force, the desire for greater policy autonomy — Quebec already has what Alberta should seek. One of the authors, Stephen Harper, now but not then the Leader of the Official Opposition in Parliament, expanded on the Quebec analogy in an earlier letter to the *National Post* written shortly after the 2000 election:

> Having hit a wall [in the 2000 election], the next logical step [for Albertans] is not to bang our heads against it. It is to take the bricks and begin building another home — a stronger and much more autonomous Alberta. It is time to look at Quebec and learn. What Albertans should take from this example is to become *"maîtres chez nous."* In one policy area after another, the province of Quebec, with much less financial independence than Alberta, has taken initiatives to ensure it is controlled by its own culture and its own majority. Such a strategy across a range of policy areas will quickly put Alberta on the cutting edge of a world where the region, the continent and the globe are becoming more important than the nation-state.[20]

For a complex variety of reasons, the firewall proposal did not ignite broad support within the province. Premier Klein, perhaps reacting to the implied criticism that he was not doing enough, was at best guarded and cool in his response. Some of the proposals, most notably the creation of a provincial pension plan and police force, were new to the Alberta public policy arena and, therefore, could not be readily absorbed without greater reflection and public debate. The hostility to Ottawa that animated the report abated somewhat as the federal government adopted a less confrontational approach to health policy reform and toned down the rhetoric that had characterized the 2000 election campaign, although this change in the political climate evaporated in 2002 as Ottawa returned to a much more heavy-handed approach, certainly so in the case of the ratification of the Kyoto Accord.

It should also be stressed that the firewall was never conceived as a *regional* strategy. It generated no enthusiasm outside Alberta where critics assumed that the firewall would be built from oil revenues they did not share. Nor, for that matter, have similar proposals been advanced for the other western Canadian provinces individually. Regional wariness of federal spending power was not sufficient to ignite support for provincial or regional firewalls.

At the core of the firewall strategy is the understandable quest for greater autonomy within an increasingly interdependent world. It is not radically different in spirit from Canada's quest for autonomous policy space within NAFTA. However, as we will discuss in Chapter 6, it is also a quest that more and more seems inspired by Don Quixote, as the weight of policy interdependence presses down on political jurisdictions around the world. Firewalls may only make sense for jurisdictions such as the United States that truly have a significant measure of policy autonomy and capacity. For better or for worse, "Fortress America" is a more attainable goal than is "Fortress Alberta."

Greater Decentralization

A more general strategy that potentially could be pursued by provincial governments across the West would be one of greater decentralization. Governments could seek constitutional amendments, a huge barrier in itself, to expand their legislative reach. It is by no means clear, however, that there is a functional case to be made for expanding as opposed to protecting the legislative jurisdiction of provincial governments. The historical record would suggest a weak case. Conflicts with the national government in the past have centred on issues falling intrinsically within the legislative domain of Parliament, such as trade policy, tariffs, freight rates, interprovincial transportation. None of these could easily be moved under the jurisdictional wing of provincial legislatures. Even in the case of the NEP, Parliament was acting within its own legislative domain, and the powers brought to bear, particularly those dealing with international trade, were not ones that could be devolved to the provinces. This is why western discontent has focused more on an effective voice in Parliament than on reducing Parliament's legislative domain. There are good reasons why the dominant call for action has been "the West wants in" rather than "the West wants a more decentralized Canada."

DIFFERENCES BETWEEN QUEBEC AND THE WEST ON DECENTRALIZATION

Greater decentralization has always made sense as a federalism strategy in Quebec. The desire to protect and preserve a distinct society can be addressed by the devolution of powers and/or by a limitation on federal intrusions into the provincial domain. The public policy issues that have mattered the most in Quebec, or at least have mattered the most to nationalists in Quebec, have been those relating to social policy and language. These are policy issues that fit neatly within the provincial realm. Western Canadians, however, have traditionally been more focused on the linkages between the West and the broader continental and global economies, and these linkages fall intrinsically to the national government. On matters of social policy, profound disputes between provincial communities in the West and the Government of Canada have been relatively rare. Thus, the West has sought greater leverage *within* the national government, something taken for granted by Quebec, where power within the national corridors of power is a given. While the two regions converge at times with respect to trying to restrict national government intrusions into the provincial realm, only Quebecers have consistently sought to increase the scope of that realm. For Quebecers, decentralization is a complement to power at the centre, whereas for western Canadians it is an alternative, and not a preferred alternative.

Even the most assertive western Canadian premiers have seldom advocated greater decentralization. To the contrary, they have been staunch defenders of the federal status quo, arguing for greater respect for the provinces' constitutionally defined legislative domain rather than an expansion of that domain. It has been federal government incursions into the provincial domain that have rankled and that have been resisted. Former Alberta Premier Peter Lougheed epitomized this approach, arguing vigorously for respect of the constitution and, more particularly, for respect of provincial ownership of natural resources. The message has been clear if not always well understood outside the region: let us manage our own affairs in a way consistent with the desires and aspirations of our provincial electorates, and let Ottawa manage its own affairs in a way consistent with the health and vitality of the national community. In short, let us respect the federal status quo rather than seek greater decentralization.

Although there appears to be considerable regional public opinion support for greater decentralization, the depth and character of this support are open to interpretation. Figure 4.5 shows that a majority of western Canadians feel that the federal government has too much power. Nonetheless, it is not clear whether this reflects a principled belief in greater decentralization or a strategic response to the tenets of western alienation, which hold that anything left in the hands of the federal government will be overspent, poorly managed, and inequitable in its regional impact. In effect, regional aversion to federal spending patterns may ripple through preferences about the division of powers. If western perceptions about the nature of federal programs could be improved, we suspect that western Canadians would not in principle support greater decentralization. In the continuing context of western alienation, however, greater decentralization is a strategy with substantial public appeal.

It should also be noted that the public policy case for greater decentralization has not been made in the West. When we get into the current policy agenda discussed in the next chapter and consider the growing degree of policy interdependence discussed in Chapter 6, there is little evidence that a stronger case can be constructed in the future. Given, then, the lack of government, electoral, and public policy support for greater decentralization, one might assume that there would be no support whatsoever within the region for separatism or political independence. This is largely, but not entirely, true.

FIGURE 4.5:   REGIONAL PERCEPTIONS OF THE BALANCE OF
FEDERAL POWERS

"In your opinion, does the federal government have too much
power, do the provincial governments have too much power,
or is the balance between them about right?"

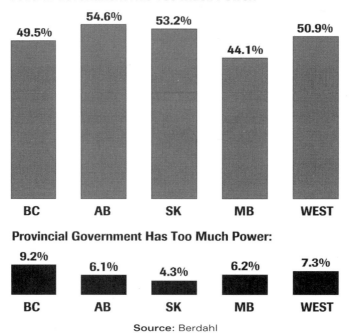

Federal Government Has Too Much Power:

BC	AB	SK	MB	WEST
49.5%	54.6%	53.2%	44.1%	50.9%

Provincial Government Has Too Much Power:

BC	AB	SK	MB	WEST
9.2%	6.1%	4.3%	6.2%	7.3%

Source: Berdahl

Variants of an Independent West

Somewhat surprisingly, calls for an independent West have been heard
repeatedly over the past three or four decades. Less surprisingly, these calls
have frequently mimicked the separatist movement in Quebec. The result
has been a spate of separatist organizations and parties, none of which has
garnered any significant degree of public support. They tend to appear
between elections and have seldom tested their support within provincial
or federal election campaigns. Still, they litter the political landscape in
the West — the Western Canada Concept, the Alberta Independence
Party, the Republic of Alberta, the One-Ten West, and others.

It must be strongly emphasized that there is no consensus model for what might constitute an independent West. Given that there are no constitutional parameters to the region analogous to the constitutional parameters for Quebec and given that there is a lack of linguistic or ethnic differentiation for the region, it is perhaps not surprising that the parameters of an independent West are ambiguous. Some separatist parties, most notably those springing up in Alberta, have been provincially based. Sometimes separatist rhetoric lumps together Alberta and British Columbia and sometimes the West as a whole, although Manitoba is the least likely province to be included. The bottom line is that there is no common understanding of what might be encompassed by an independent West. The image remains an abstraction without identified boundaries much less a potential site for the new national capital.

A WESTERN "KNIFE AT THE THROAT"

The argument for a western separatist movement is often a strategic argument based on Quebec's assumed success in using the threat of separatism to extract concessions from Ottawa. This is a strategic approach that is emphatically rejected by *Vancouver Sun* columnist Barbara Yaffe:

"The best available option is to keep fighting politically, keep choosing the most powerful political voices available — representing either the government or opposition side — and dispatching them to Ottawa.

While separatist groups serve a purpose, as they have in Quebec in holding a knife to the federal throat, surely this isn't the way the West wants to do business. . . . Separatism has been a nightmare for Quebec, dangerously dividing Quebecers and bringing lengthy periods of economic stagnation and uncertainty which have discouraged investment.

So fixated is Quebec's population on the separation stalemate, other important policy issues are regularly neglected. Is this the future westerners want? As someone who grew up with the separatist movement and ultimately left Quebec in large measure because of it, I can only warn in the strongest terms possible against a similar strategy for the West."[21]

There is also no clear understanding, or even a murky understanding, of how an independent West would position itself *vis-à-vis* the rest of Canada. The long and largely unfruitful Quebec debate on models of sovereignty association has had no parallel in the West. Neither has the possible relationship with the northern territories been explored. And, perhaps most importantly, there has been little serious exploration of potential relationships with the United States. Would western separatism be a stepping-stone to integration with the United States? Would there be any American interest? To some degree, the potential relationship between at least part of an independent West — British Columbia and perhaps Alberta — and the United States has been addressed in discussions of Cascadia. This notion, however, is ill-defined in itself. Its geographic scope is unclear — the watershed surrounding Vancouver and Seattle? The West coast running from Oregon to Alaska? — as is the nature of the community. Cascadia is sometimes seen as a prototypical political community, but at other times it appears to be little more than an ecological frame of mind.

There has been little discussion of whether an independent West, much less independent provincial communities, would make sense within the continental context of North America and globalization. The West as a whole has a population not much larger than that of the San Francisco Bay area in California, and Alberta's population alone is roughly equivalent to San Diego County. Are these sufficient population bases to sustain independent political communities or national economies? Perhaps in some contexts, but not necessarily within the North American context, which is the one that counts.

It is safe to say that an independent West, or for that matter an independent Alberta and/or British Columbia, is not on the current political agenda. Separatist movements have attracted few supporters, virtually no electoral support, and no endorsement from community or political elites within the region. As the discussion in Chapter 3 illustrated, public opinion support for independence is extremely shallow. Rhetorical support for independence can best be seen as an extreme expression of western alienation. It is a statement of frustration rather than a model of a positive future vision toward which western Canada might move. It is, in part, a strategic response to what are perceived to be the benefits that Quebec has wrested from Ottawa through the threat posed by its nationalist movement. It is frustration that Quebec, with a smaller population than the West, is able to command the ear and purse of the national government. It is many things, but it is nowhere near a fully developed strategy for dealing with western alienation. It also flies in the face of W.L. Morton's introduction to this chapter: equality has been sought "in order that the West should be like, not different from the rest of Canada." And by *like* we mean an equal partner in Confederation, respected for the values and beliefs that the West brings to the national community.

Conclusions

Western alienation is a chronic condition within the Canadian body politic, one that impairs both regional and national prosperity. Given the persistence of the problem and both the demographic and economic weight of the West within Canada, it is a problem that should be addressed. To this point, the Government of Canada has not explicitly, never mind effectively, addressed the problem. It is time, therefore — indeed, well past time — that the federal government become engaged. The costs of disengagement are simply too high. However, we do not recommend new programs directed explicitly at the West, nor increased federal expenditures targeted to the West. Such initiatives would be more likely to increase rather than moderate western alienation. Rather, we recommend that the Government of Canada and the party animating that government:

- explicitly recognize both the seriousness of regional discontent and the contribution, current and potential, of western Canada to the national economy and community;

- adopt a principled approach to programming and expenditures that would ensure regional equity and fairness;
- pursue a more collaborative approach to provincial governments in the West, one that respects provincial fields of jurisdiction; and
- pursue *national* policies that the western Canadian electorate supports.

Benign neglect should be abandoned in favour of active engagement. Without such engagement, national policy objectives will be impaired.

It is also essential that provincial governments in the West become engaged in finding effective strategies to combat western alienation. As we have argued in this chapter, effective strategies are unlikely to be based on the premise of further disengagement from the national community, even through such modest steps as greater constitutional decentralization or firewall strategies. There is more hope for strategies based on active engagement across a wide front. However, an understanding of those strategies, of their strengths and limitations, first requires an understanding of the policy challenges and opportunities facing western Canadians in the years ahead. It is to those that we now turn.

Notes

[1] W.L. Morton, "The Bias of Prairie Politics," *Transactions of the Royal Society of Canada*, Series III, 49 (June 1955): Section II, 66.

[2] For a detailed discussion of changing trade patterns in western Canada see Robert Roach, *Beyond Our Borders: Western Canadian Exports in the Global Market* (Calgary, AB: Canada West Foundation, May 2002).

[3] Data for the rest of Canada reflect Ontario's high degree of integration into the continental economy, a degree that far exceeds that of any other province.

[4] An argument can be made, moreover, that sub-national identities are likely to become more rather than less important in the wake of globalization. See Harmsworth.

[5] The non-governmental sector, including both business and community groups, also has a role to play in addressing regional grievances and, especially, regional aspirations.

[6] The 2001 Census showed that for the 1996-2001 period, immigration overtook births as the country's primary source of population growth.

[7] Western Economic Diversification website, <www.wd.gc.ca>.

[8] Atlantic Canada Opportunities Agency website, <www.acoa.ca>.

[9] *Saskatoon Star Phoenix* 8 March 2002: A11.

[10] Barbara Yaffe, "Ottawa finds yet another way to ruin Canadian businesses," *Calgary Herald* 6 March 2002: A13.

[11] Norm Ovenden, "West feels left out of Canada," *Calgary Herald* 19 December 2000: A1.

[12] David E. Smith, "Party Government, Representation and National Integration in Canada," *Party Government and Regional Representation in Canada*, ed. Peter Aucoin (Toronto, ON: University of Toronto Press, 1985) 51.

[13] Alan C. Cairns, "The Electoral System and the Party System in Canada, 1921-1965," *Canadian Journal of Political Science* 1, 1 (March 1968): 55–80.

[14] This redistribution will happen, but not necessarily before the next general election.

[15] For example, see the Law Commission of Canada, *Renewing Democracy: Debating Electoral Reform in Canada* (Ottawa, ON: Law Commission of Canada, 2002).

[16] *Calgary Herald* 27 January 2001: A4.

[17] The authors of the open letter were Stephen Harper, then president of the National Citizens' Coalition and now leader of the Canadian Alliance; Tom Flanagan, professor of political science at the University of Calgary and former director of research for the Reform Party; Ted Morton, professor of political science at the University of Calgary and Alberta senator-elect; Rainer Knopff, professor of political science at the University of Calgary; Andrew Crooks, chairman of the Canadian Taxpayers Federation; and Ken Boessenkool, former policy advisor to former Alberta Treasurer and Leader of the Official Opposition, Stockwell Day.

[18] Unlike the situation in Ontario and Quebec, the RCMP provides police services for those parts of Alberta lying outside the major metropolitan areas.

[19] Howard May, "New group to push for Alberta autonomy," *Calgary Herald* 27 January 2001: A4.

[20] Stephen Harper, "Separation, Alberta-style," *National Post* 8 December 2000: A18.

[21] Barbara Yaffe, "Separation a recipe for stagnation," *Calgary Herald* 8 January 2001: A10.

CHAPTER 5

BUILDING THE NEW WEST:
Forging the Policy Environment

"Canada is so diverse that it is impossible to have an economic policy that fits the needs of all the regions; it is better by far to break it down into a regional approach."[1]

—FORMER MANITOBA PREMIER GARY FILMON

Introduction

Regional conflicts, and for that matter federal-provincial and partisan conflicts, seldom take place in the abstract. They are generally grounded in competing interests and aspirations and expressed through disputes over specific policy issues. Even if the underlying conflict is generic, such as the conflict among political parties as they compete for electoral support, its manifestations are linked to specific public policies. One party does not simply label its opponents as bad or undesirable; they are bad or undesirable *because* of the policy stance they take towards particular issues. The Canadian Alliance, for example, is attacked by the Liberals on the basis of its policies towards national unity (too much of that "better regional representation" stuff), privatization, and international refugees, while the Liberals are attacked by the Canadian Alliance for their policies with respect to government spending, public sector management, and taxation. The same conclusion applies to both intergovernmental conflict and collaboration — we look for evidence of either in terms of how specific public policy issues are handled. It matters less whether governments fight or collaborate in general than it does how they handle particular issues such as health care.

This means, then, that a full understanding of regional conflict in the West, of western alienation and the opportunities for cooperation on the national stage, requires an appreciation of the regional policy agenda. If we are to identify the potential flashpoints and prospects for cooperative collaboration, we need to know the issues likely to dominate the West's, and indeed the nation's, policy agenda. In this respect it is also essential to look well down the road, past short-term policy concerns and crises. As the expression "next year country" suggests, western Canadians are relatively optimistic and forward looking. Although they are clearly unhappy with the federalism status quo, and although this underlying dissatisfaction can easily be attached to a broad range of issues, on a daily basis western Canadians are more likely to engage in discussions about the future of their city, province, or region than they are to focus on past grievances. They look for ways to build from existing successes and to ensure long-term regional prosperity and well-being. To the extent that the themes of western alienation come into play, they provide both important context — the National Energy Program, for example, provides a regional lens for discussions about the Kyoto Accord — and a set of policy challenges and constraints that must be addressed in the pursuit of regional prosperity.

As we will see, the regional policy agenda in western Canada shares a good deal in common with the national policy agenda, something that should not be surprising given the West's share of the national population and economy. Nonetheless, the same issues can play out quite differently in different regional contexts and, for that matter, in different provincial contexts across the West. Therefore, to raise western Canadian policy issues is not to assert that such issues are necessarily unique to, or play out uniformly across, the region. Often they are not and do not. Nor, however, should it be assumed that regional policy issues can be approached satisfactorily through cookie-cutter national programs or even that a regional perspective makes sense for all issues. The task is first to identify policy priorities and then determine the extent to which national, regional, or provincial frames should be applied.

But what lies ahead for the western Canadian policy agenda? What will the next few years or decades bring? To answer these questions we must turn to the broad demographic, economic, and political trends already shaping the region. By doing so, we can begin to get a sense of future options, of where public policies might have some leverage and where that leverage may be slight. (While no trends are immovable, some are extremely resistant to the influence of public policy.) When planning for regional prosperity and well-being, long-term trends provide the starting point for constructive public policy debate.

Demographic Trends in Western Canada

Six demographic trends are of particular significance when considering the future of western Canada. Although they are by no means unique to the West, they interweave and interact within the region to create a policy environment that is in many ways distinct.

Uneven Population Growth

As noted in Chapter 1, western Canada's share of the national population has modestly increased over the past 30 years, and at the time of the 2001 Census stood at just under 30 per cent. However, growth has not been evenly spread across the region. As Figure 5.1 shows, recent growth has occurred primarily in British Columbia and Alberta, with growth rates in Manitoba and Saskatchewan remaining relatively flat. If we look only at growth between 1996 and 2001, the period spanning the two most recent national censuses, Alberta grew by 10.3 per cent and British Columbia by 4.9 per cent, while Manitoba grew by only 0.5 per cent, and Saskatchewan's population actually declined by 1.1 per cent. To put this picture into a broader historical perspective, the populations of Manitoba and Saskatchewan have increased by only 60 and 6 per cent respectively since the 1931 Census, whereas the populations of Alberta and British Columbia have grown by 307 and 463 per cent respectively over the same period.

FIGURE 5.1:   INTRA-REGIONAL POPULATION GROWTH, 1971 TO 2001

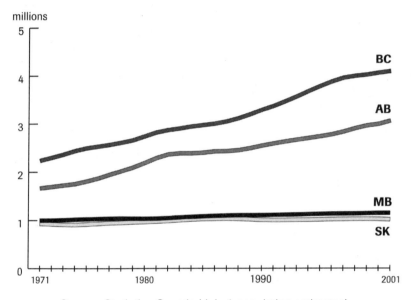

Source: Statistics Canada (July 1 population estimates)

The mix of population growth and decline is by no means unique to the West. In the 1996 to 2001 period, for example, Nova Scotia, New Brunswick, and Newfoundland all experienced population declines, whereas Ontario grew substantially. In fact, over those five years Ontario's population increased by 656,000, an incremental gain equal to the combined populations of Newfoundland and Prince Edward Island. (Ontario grew by the equivalent of the Yukon or Nunavut every ten weeks.) Nor are we implying that population growth is uniformly a good thing or that stable populations are inherently problematic. To argue that Saskatchewan would necessarily provide a better quality of life or higher standard of living for its residents if it were home to two million rather than one million people is an argument that has to be made with a great deal of care; the correlation between population growth and economic prosperity is far from perfect. Nevertheless, in popular discourse there is little doubt that growth is seen as a marker for prosperity and that stagnant or declining populations are seen as a cause for alarm. No premier hoping for re-election would appear before the media to praise the virtues of a declining provincial population.

The substantial differences in population growth among the four western provinces are hugely important for the regional policy agenda, for they speak to a significant public policy divide falling along the Saskatchewan/Alberta border. Population growth brings with it an increased tax base, a larger labour supply, economic stimulation, an expanded consumer market, increased national "clout," and a general sense of optimism. In all of these respects, uneven population growth within the region points to growing disparities among the four western provinces — in a sense, an east-west divide within western Canada itself. British Columbia and Alberta seek to manage growth and maximize its benefits, while Manitoba and Saskatchewan seek to limit depopulation and encourage growth.

Demographers estimate that western Canada's population growth will continue to be uneven in the years ahead. For example, Statistics Canada projects population decline in Saskatchewan and very modest population growth in Manitoba over the next 25 years, while significant growth in the two western-most provinces is likely to continue. This demographic divide will ripple through a host of public policy issues, and it is immediately apparent when we turn to population mobility within the West. For the region as a whole, policy makers and political leaders must grapple with the fact that, to a significant degree, population growth west of the Alberta/Saskatchewan divide is cannibalizing the regional population base east of that divide. Those most affected, moreover, tend to be the best and the brightest, young western Canadians with the educational credentials essential for success in the knowledge-based economy.

Youth Mobility

There has been growing debate in recent years about the "brain drain." Most of those voicing concerns look south of the border, to American companies perceived to be hiring away our "best and brightest," generally defined as those possessing both youth and postsecondary educations. Not only is this alarm vaguely insulting to those of us who continue to live in Canada — as Mordecai Richler implied, apparently only the mediocre and dull remain — but it misrepresents Canada's true mobility patterns. Interprovincial mobility is more pronounced than is the brain drain to the United States. Young people and university graduates are much more likely to move east or west than head south. And, when they do move, their movement is not random. There are clear provincial winners and losers.[2]

THE UPSIDE OF THE BRAIN DRAIN

Mordecai Richler wrote that the harmful effects of the brain drain on the Canadian economy might be overstated. The "....burgeoning brain drainage needn't have significant negative repercussions here. Au contraire. Good riddance! Look here, the more brainy types who quit the country, the more opportunities there are for the rest of us second-raters. So clap hands for brain drainage, if only because it gives Canadian mediocrity a real chance."[3]

This is apparent in western Canada where the region's economic history is written on the record of interprovincial migration. As noted in Chapter 1, almost 500,000 more Canadians moved into the West than left over the past 30 years. It is important to stress, however, that each of the four provinces has had a very different history of population churn. As Figure 5.2 illustrates, with only a few exceptions British Columbia has experienced a net inflow from interprovincial migration over the past 30 years. Although the provincial economy has undergone some major fluctuations during this time, interprovincial migration tends to stick to the West Coast. Alberta's record has been quite different; people move into the province when times are good and move out when times are bad. This was particularly evident from the early 1980s to the mid-1990s when poor energy prices and a general economic downturn (one factor being the NEP) resulted in buildings abandoned mid-construction and a proliferation of "for rent" and "for sale" signs. In Saskatchewan and Manitoba, the pattern has been different again. In both cases, the past three decades have been marked by steady out-migration. Year in and year out, more people leave these provinces than arrive from elsewhere in Canada.

FIGURE 5.2: INTERPROVINCIAL MIGRATION IN WESTERN CANADA, 1972-1999

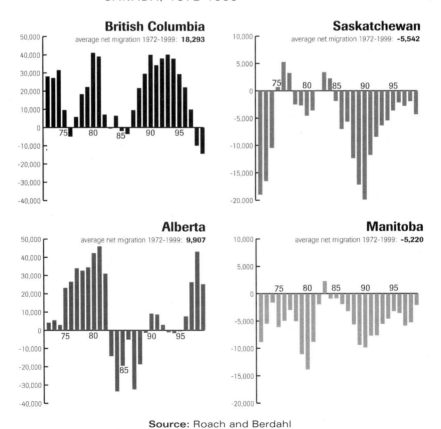

Source: Roach and Berdahl

Who are the migrants? Not surprisingly, those most likely to move come from two interconnected social groupings: the young and the well-educated. People are most mobile when they are relatively young (18-34 years of age). As people age, they typically get married, have children, and buy homes — in short, they lay down solid roots in their communities; thus, the social costs associated with mobility increase. The highly educated, particularly young people with bachelor, graduate, or professional degrees, are also more likely to move given that employment prospects increase with education.

Youth mobility will grow rather than decline in the years ahead. Many of the emotional reasons for staying in one's home city or province have been weakened by the availability of e-mail, affordable long-distance telephone plans, and rapid air service. Interprovincial barriers with respect to the transfer of skills, although still present and problematic, are lower than they have been in years past. In short, young people have more incentives and fewer barriers to move to the province and, more likely, to the city that offers them the best opportunities for career advancement and a high quality of life. And young people are aware of the potential for mobility. In the 2001 Canada West survey (Figure 5.3), it was found that one in five western Canadians between the ages of 18 and 24 anticipates moving out of their province within five years. For the province of Saskatchewan, this figure jumps to an astonishing 40 per cent, speaking to negative perceptions of the province's economic future. It should also be noted that students across the region — regardless of age — are more likely than non-students to anticipate moving. Given that the western provinces will need to attract and retain young, educated people in the years ahead in order to remain competitive, youth and student mobility present a challenge, particularly for Saskatchewan and Manitoba.

The Canada West survey also demonstrates that interprovincial mobility is more of a social reality than is the brain drain to the United States. Young people are much more willing to move to another Canadian province for economic opportunities (79 per cent willing to

FIGURE 5.3:   YOUTH EXPECTATIONS WITH RESPECT TO
               MOBILITY

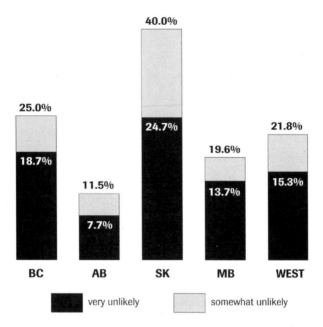

Source: Berdahl

move) than they are to the United States (52 per cent willing to move). Thus, Canadian provinces have a significant "home ice advantage" in attracting young people. That said, the 52 per cent willing to consider a move to the United States is not a small number; the fact that over one in two are willing to leave Canada for better economic opportunities in the United States represents a considerable threat. All told, the mobility data reinforce the fact that western Canadian provinces need to compete — with each other, with central and eastern Canadian provinces, and with the United States and other countries — to retain and attract well-educated youth. What is less clear, but of vital importance nonetheless, is the appropriate mix of national, provincial, and municipal public policies needed to strengthen both the retention and attraction of human capital without choking off the mobility necessary for economic growth and vitality.

In drawing this discussion to a close, it is important to stress that mobility per se is not necessarily a problem. The movement of human capital *within the country* is in many ways a measure of economic strength and adaptability. Mobility contributes significantly to an agile and innovative economy. It is also a sign of social strength when individuals seek to play upon a national stage, to consider their careers and lives in a national context, unconstrained by provincial borders. "Don't fence me in" is not a bad individual and national creed. Relatively high rates of interprovincial mobility may even strengthen national unity by giving Canadians a broader perspective on their country and a broader set of truly national experiences. Finally, it is important to note a key difference between interprovincial migration and the brain drain to the United States. If a young person decides to leave Saskatoon for Calgary, she is not lost to the *Canadian* economy. Indeed, the national economy may benefit from her willingness to move. If, on the other hand, she decides to leave Saskatoon for Los Angeles, she is lost to the Canadian economy, as is the public investment in her education and training. The fact that interprovincial mobility is far more prevalent than international mobility should not conceal the very real costs associated with the latter.

At the same time, significant net differences in interprovincial population flows do raise important public policy challenges. For example, and for example only, if Saskatchewan universities are in effect training graduates for a national rather than a provincial labour market, this raises questions as to whether the costs of those universities should be borne by Saskatchewan taxpayers or by Canadian taxpayers at large. More generally, Canadian public policies in the past have been designed as a countervail to market forces encouraging mobility; that is what regional economic development programs are all about. (Note the mandates of ACOA and, to a lesser extent, WD.) It is unlikely in the near future that Canadians and their governments will abandon a tradition of trying to move jobs to people rather than encouraging people to follow employment opportunities across provincial lines. However, whether this dedication is conducive to regional and national prosperity is by no means clear.

Population Aging

Population aging is not unique to western Canada, or even to the whole country: it is a demographic phenomenon that is being experienced to varying degrees across the developed world. Population aging is caused by two key changes in fertility patterns over the past decades. First, women are having fewer children. Canada's fertility rate has dropped from 3.8 in 1960 to a record low of 1.52 in 1999, a rate well below that needed for population replacement. Second, women are tending to give birth at an older age; the average age of a Canadian woman having her first child is now nearly 29 years.[4] This delayed childbearing pattern means that it now takes longer for the generations to replace themselves — generations are now closer to 30 years rather than 20 years apart.

The global reach of the aging phenomenon does not make it any less of a challenge for western Canada. Between 1981 and 2000, the number of western Canadians over age 65 grew by 59 per cent, topping out at over 12 per cent of the population (1.1 million seniors). By 2025, it is estimated that 21 per cent of the region's population will be over age 65. Although the proportion of seniors is growing across the West, once again there are significant interprovincial differences. Alberta currently has the lowest proportion of seniors, although this gap is projected to close in the years ahead, bringing Alberta in line with the other western provinces. At the present time, however, Alberta is blessed with a favourable demography, with a relatively high proportion of the provincial population in the labour force. Despite British Columbia's reputation as a retirement province, the province does not have an unusually high proportion of seniors relative to its regional partners; its demographic profile is not radically different from that of Alberta.

It is in Saskatchewan and Manitoba that we find the highest proportion of seniors. The Saskatchewan case with respect to population aging is particularly interesting because it illustrates the compounding effects of interprovincial migration. If the young are the most likely to move, and if they are most likely to move to Alberta or British Columbia, then the aging of Saskatchewan's population will be accelerated at the same time that the provinces to the west are being infused with relatively young migrants. It is difficult to put a good spin on this for Saskatchewan's labour force and tax base.

FIGURE 5.4:   POPULATION AGING IN WESTERN CANADA

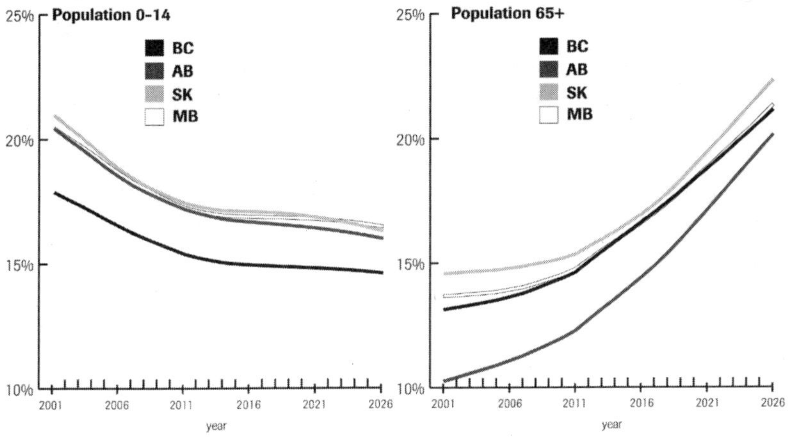

Source: Roach and Berdahl

Although fertility patterns and population aging are difficult to alter through public policy, they do have significant public policy implications. Population aging means that there are fewer and fewer "natural born" individuals available to fulfill labour market needs; that the tax base is declining while dependency ratios grow; and that, as Figure 5.5 illustrates, health care costs climb higher over time. Interprovincial differences in the age profile of the population thus carry significant implications with respect to economic competition among the four western provinces. Those blessed with a favourable demography have greater labour force participation rates, lower dependency rates, and a stronger tax base. While demography may not be destiny, it is a good predictor of economic performance and social costs.

FIGURE 5.5:   PER CAPITA PROVINCIAL HEALTH COSTS BY
AGE GROUP, 1998

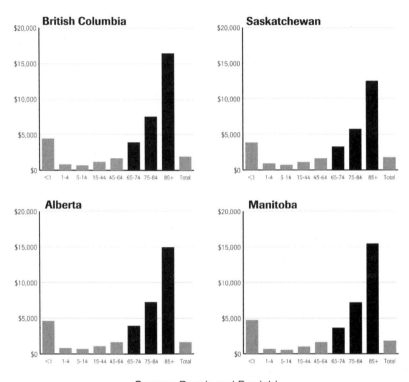

Source: Roach and Berdahl

THE CHALLENGE OF ALTERING
FERTILITY PATTERNS

Some would argue that the solution to population aging can be found in public policy incentives to encourage larger families and earlier parenthood. Indeed, a number of countries have moved in this direction, or have at least raised the idea of "baby bonuses" in national election campaigns. To provide but one example, in 2001 Singapore implemented a "Baby Bonus Scheme" that provides parents with $500 per year for six years for the first child and $1,000 per year for six years for the second and third child. Singapore's Baby Bonus Scheme also allows for co-savings (with governments matching parents dollar for dollar up to an annual capped amount) for payment of government-approved day cares, registered kindergartens, and special education schools.[5]

Should Canada's federal or provincial governments adopt pro-natal policies to encourage larger family sizes in order to ensure our long-term labour needs? Although the answer is not clear, it is probably no. First, the jury is still out as to whether such policies are effective in reversing fertility patterns. The reality is that Canada's societal norms are highly biased towards smaller families and delayed parenting; given that family planning is such an important individual choice, it is questionable to what extent modest financial incentives will have an impact. Second, if a pro-natal policy is successful, it will result in a temporary removal of a large number of young people — primarily women — from the labour market for a one-to-five year period for the purposes of parenting. In this way, pro-natal policies weigh long-term labour needs above short-term labour needs — a politically difficult move with considerable short-term consequences for the regional economy.

Growing Importance of Immigration

The discussion of population aging takes us immediately to the growing importance of immigration. The 2001 Census shows that, for the first time ever, immigration has surpassed births as the primary driver of population growth. Canada, therefore, will need to be successful in attracting and retaining immigrants within an increasingly competitive global marketplace if we are to avoid depopulation in the years ahead. Governments and businesses across the country are certainly aware of the growing importance of immigration for maintaining our labour pool and tax base. Although increased immigration alone will not be sufficient to meet the demographic challenge, it is a necessary component of any national, regional, or provincial human capital strategy. Immigration is also seen as the means by which Canada can compensate for the brain drain to the United States, although there is considerable dispute about the net effects of immigration into and emigration from Canada.[6]

Although the immigration challenges that Canada faces are national in scope, they play out quite differently across the regions. The growing importance of immigration comes as mixed news for western Canada. Although the region was very successful in attracting immigrants during the heyday of agrarian settlement, a success driven in large part by an aggressive national immigration strategy, the West in recent decades has not been attracting its proportionate share of international immigrants. It has received 27 per cent of all immigrants (3 per cent less than its national population weight), a share that holds up well against Quebec and the Atlantic provinces but lags Ontario. Moreover, immigrants are not proportionately dispersed across the region. As Figure 5.6 shows, most of western Canada's immigrants go to British Columbia, more specifically to Vancouver. Thus, British Columbia, with less than half of the region's population, attracts almost two-thirds of new immigrants. Despite its economic prosperity, Alberta is not attracting its proportionate share of international immigrants, although it may be getting a second immigration "bounce" through interprovincial migration. Saskatchewan and Manitoba face the most serious challenge in attracting and retaining immigrants.

One might assume, falling back on "the West as redneck country" stereotypes, that part of the explanation for poor immigrant attraction on the Prairies is hostile or negative public attitudes. However, surveys of attitudes toward immigration do not bear this out. For example, in a 2000 Angus Reid survey conducted for a national conference on immigration,[7] Saskatchewan and Manitoba respondents had more favourable attitudes toward increasing immigration levels than did respondents in British Columbia, Ontario, Quebec, or Atlantic Canada. Albertans were the least favourably disposed to immigration, but it is important to note that Alberta attitudes have been improving over time. As the Canada West 2001 survey data in Figure 5.7 demonstrate, Alberta attitudes are approaching those of its neighbouring provinces. As public awareness of the policy challenges resulting from population aging increases, attitudes toward immigration across the

FIGURE 5.6:   PROVINCIAL DISTRIBUTION OF INTERNATIONAL IMMIGRANTS TO WESTERN CANADA, 1999

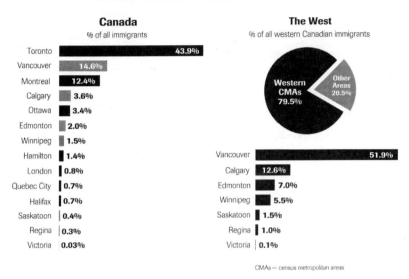

Source: Roach and Berdahl

FIGURE 5.7:   PUBLIC OPINION SUPPORT FOR INCREASES IN IMMIGRATION, 2001

Do you think Canada should accept more immigrants, fewer immigrants, or about the same number we accept now?

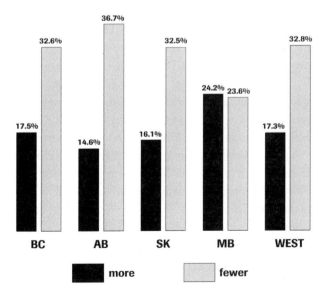

Source: Berdahl

country will hopefully improve. At the same time, the long-term impact of the September 11 terrorist attacks on North American attitudes towards immigration is still unknown.

The immigration data show once again how demographic trends in western Canada can be mutually reinforcing. Relatively high rates of immigration intake are associated with relatively high rates of interprovincial migration intake and young populations. The provinces that gain with respect to one indicator gain with respect to them all, just as the provinces that lose with respect to one lose with respect to them all. International immigration does not offset population losses occurring from the outflow of interprovincial migration. To the contrary, interprovincial differences in attracting immigration simply compound interprovincial differences in domestic mobility. The upshot is that the demographic divide within the West gets only deeper as we move from one indicator to the next. This pattern continues when we turn to the Aboriginal population.

Aboriginal Population Growth

The Aboriginal population is of great significance to western Canada. As noted in Chapter 1, the West is home to two-thirds of Canada's Aboriginal population, and this population is growing both absolutely and relative to the non-Aboriginal population. A number of population projections suggest that Aboriginal population growth will continue at a rapid rate. For example, the analysis used for the Royal Commission on Aboriginal Peoples projects that, in 2016, western Canada's Aboriginal population will reach 688,000, assuming medium growth rates and current migration patterns.[8] A 1997 Manitoba Bureau of Statistics Study projected that Manitoba's Aboriginal population will grow to 192,000 (over 15 per cent of the projected Manitoba population) by 2016.[9] While economists and demographers may differ over the exact assumptions used for projections, all predict growth rates for the Aboriginal population well in excess of non-Aboriginal growth rates.

Given population aging and the prairie West's limited recent success in attracting immigrants, this young Aboriginal population presents an important opportunity. It is a demographic plus in a sea of demographic negatives, particularly for Saskatchewan and Manitoba. The large number of Aboriginal youth have the potential to significantly strengthen the human capital base of the regional economy and augment the tax base.[10] However, for western Canada and Aboriginal people alike to realize this potential, the existing gaps between the Aboriginal and general populations in terms of labour market participation and employment rates must be closed or, at the very least, narrowed. At the time of the 1996 Census, 57.5 per cent of the Aboriginal population in western Canada was participating in the labour market, compared to 68.3 per cent of the regional population at large. The lower participation rate for Aboriginal peoples was compounded by much higher unemployment rates — 24.4 per cent compared to only 8.3 per cent for the total regional population.[11]

In addition, the relationship between the Aboriginal and non-Aboriginal communities must be framed in a positive and constructive manner. Unfortunately, as Figure 5.8 illustrates, the 2001 Canada West survey found that almost one-third of western Canadians feel this relationship is deteriorating. If these perceptions are true, this presents a significant challenge for the region. It is encouraging to note, however, that the most positive perceptions are to be found in Saskatchewan and Manitoba, the two provinces with the largest proportions of Aboriginal peoples.

It is difficult to overstate the importance of Aboriginal affairs to the future of western Canada. Although no region of the country is untouched by the very complex and far too frequently acrimonious relationship between Aboriginal peoples and the broader Canadian society, no region is touched as much as the West. The size of the Aboriginal population, the geographical scope of treaties, the proximity of Aboriginal communities to resource developments, and the unsettled treaty environment in British Columbia all give an urgency to

FIGURE 5.8:   REGIONAL PERCEPTIONS OF THE
                    ABORIGINAL/NON-ABORIGINAL RELATIONSHIP

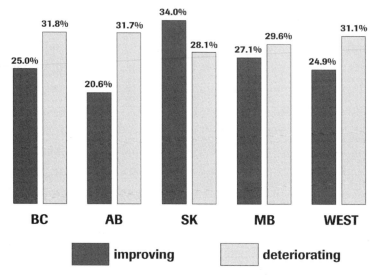

Do you think relations between Aboriginal peoples and other Canadians are
improving, deteriorating, or staying about the same?

Source: Berdahl

Aboriginal affairs that is unmatched elsewhere in the country, apart
perhaps for the northern territories. At stake is not only the prosperity
of Aboriginal communities, but the prosperity of the region itself.

It should also be noted that the Aboriginal population in western
Canada is increasingly urban. In fact, at the time of the 2001 Census,
more than 50 per cent of the Aboriginal population lived in urban
centers. As a consequence, Aboriginal affairs have become closely linked
to an emerging and critically important urban agenda in western
Canada. The interface and interplay between the Aboriginal and non-
Aboriginal communities now takes place not only in often remote
Aboriginal communities and resource developments, but in the West's
urban heartland.

Continued Urbanization

Popular images of western Canada are unfailingly rural: majestic mountains, endless prairie wheat fields, northern lakes, and wine country. These images are correct for the landmass, but they are extremely inaccurate when thinking about the population of the region. The rural West lives on primarily in the mythology of a region that is experiencing the same rate of urbanization as the rest of Canada and, on most measures, is as urbanized as any region in the country. Even the *relatively* rural provinces of Saskatchewan and Manitoba are becoming increasingly urban, with urban growth offset by rural depopulation in Saskatchewan. (In Alberta, by contrast, rapid urban growth has been accompanied by real population growth in rural areas even though the rural component of the provincial population is declining in relative terms.) Over the past 35 years the pace of urbanization has increased, outstripping the rate in other parts of the country. As a consequence, the "new West" is emphatically an urban West.

The fastest growing parts of western Canada are the large city-regions. Between 1966 and 1996, for example, Calgary, Edmonton, and Vancouver all doubled in size. Given the differences in population growth across the four western provinces, it comes as no surprise that the fastest growing cities are to be found in the western half of the region. Table 5.1 places the major western Canadian cities within the context of the country's 27 census metropolitan areas. As the table shows, three of Canada's five fastest growing metropolitan areas in the 1996-2001 period were in Alberta and British Columbia. (Vancouver is Canada's third largest census metropolitan area while Calgary is fifth, Edmonton is sixth, and Winnipeg is eighth.) Growth in Regina, Saskatoon, and Winnipeg was much more modest and, indeed, was negative in Regina.

Overall, the urbanization of the West, and particularly the growth of the large city-regions, is a highly positive trend. Large cities are increasingly recognized as key economic drivers, particularly in the new knowl-

FIGURE 5.9:   PERCENT CHANGE IN URBAN AND RURAL
POPULATIONS, 1966-2001

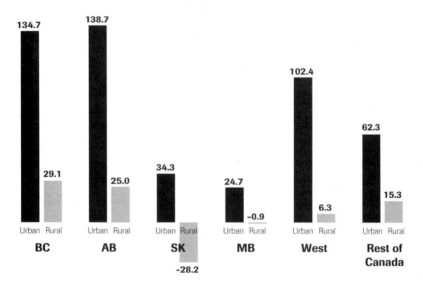

Source: Canada West Foundation

TABLE 5.1   POPULATION GROWTH IN CENSUS
METROPOLITAN AREAS, 1996-2001

CENSUS METROPOLITAN AREA	% CHANGE, 1996-2001	RANK AMONG 27 CMAs
Calgary	15.8	1
Oshawa	10.2	2
Toronto	9.8	3
Edmonton	8.7	4
Vancouver	8.5	5
Abbotsford	8.0	7
Saskatoon	3.1	13
Victoria	2.5	16
Winnipeg	0.6	20
Regina	-0.4	21

Source: Statistics Canada (July 1 population estimates)

edge-based economy, and on their future rests the region's competitive
position within the continental and global economies. However, urban

growth is not cost-free, and public policy questions will increasingly be raised about sustainability, quality of life, and the political role of the major cities in both provincial and federal politics. Conflict between the urban areas and the rural countryside can be expected to intensify, deepening yet another line of cleavage within the regional community.

The potential and challenges of urbanization and the growing prominence of large cities in our economic, political, and social life are by no means unique to the West. In this case, the West reflects and exemplifies a national pattern. It is important, therefore, that the West not be marginalized in the growing national debate on the role of cities.

Public Policy Implications of Demographic Trends

Taken together, do these six demographic trends point to any clear directions for public policy in western Canada? A number of recommendations bubble to the surface. First, the West must revamp its public policy frameworks to adapt to the reality of labour under-supply. The region faces a future of labour supply shortages and a declining number of taxpayers relative to service users. To avoid stress on the economy and to sustain funding for government programs, the four western provinces must focus on human capital development. Simply put, the West needs to retain its current human capital (young people and its educated population), attract new residents (immigrants and interprovincial migrants), and increase Aboriginal engagement in education and the labour force. Governments in the region also need to find incentives to encourage older western Canadians to stay engaged, even on a part-time basis, in the work force. This focus on human capital means a dramatic shift from public policy thinking of the past. Canada's labour system is based on the assumption of over-supply of labour. This is seen in the structuring of pensions, the allowance of mandatory retirement, the terms of most union contract agreements, and numerous other policy areas. While this assumption may have been appropriate in the past, it could not be more inappropriate for current and future realities.

The second direction that becomes apparent from the demographic trends is the need for the West to become more aggressive in the national and international competition for human capital. Western Canada is not the only region facing demographic challenges; indeed, Canada is not the only country in the world facing these challenges. Many other developed countries are actively seeking to attract immigrants — immigrants that Canada is hoping to attract and Canadians willing to emigrate for economic opportunities. The competition for human capital will grow more fierce in the years ahead, and western Canada cannot sit passively by and expect to meet its goals.

What would aggressively competing for human capital mean in a practical sense? It will require ensuring that tax rates — provincial, municipal, and, to the extent that the West can have some influence, federal — are competitive with other countries, particularly the United States. It will require re-examining western Canada's tax mix — sales, corporate income, personal income, excise, and property taxes — to ensure that the tax structures are nationally and internationally competitive. It will require ensuring a diversified economy, so that educated young people can apply their skills within the region, rather than needing to move to Toronto or Seattle. It will require reducing barriers to immigrant engagement in the labour market, barriers such as poor recognition of professional skills from other countries and inadequate English as a second language (ESL) programs. It will mean working to ensure that western Canada's cities are highly attractive, livable, and diverse centres, where young people and immigrants would like to stay. And it will mean improving the ability of Canadians to transfer their skills across the provinces. Despite the stated goals of the Agreement on Internal Trade, interprovincial barriers in skills transferability remain a national problem and embarrassment.

In most of these respects, the regional public policy agenda is very much in line with the national policy agenda, although there are some components, such as the more effective engagement of Aboriginal peoples in the labour force, that carry greater weight in the West. For the most part, however, regional and national goals are in sync; therefore, national policies and programs have the potential of serving or at least complementing regional goals. At the same time, it is important to recognize two basic realities. First, the development of human capital takes us to the core provincial responsibilities for education, health care, and social services. Thus, federal program activity runs a risk of generating federal-provincial conflict. The second is that the competition for human capital takes place within Canada as well, thereby creating the potential for inter-regional conflict. The critical issue in this regard is to ensure that the federal government is neutral in the inter-regional competition for human capital and that it recognizes that inter-regional flows and transfers are not necessarily detrimental to the performance of the national economy. Unfortunately, past experience has given western Canadians ample grounds for wariness in this respect. The assumption that the regional prosperity of the West is an essential driver of national economic prosperity is not one that can be taken for granted within the context of the national government.

Economic Trends in Western Canada

Along with the rest of North America, western Canada was on an economic upswing for the latter half of the 1990s and the early 2000s. Fortunately, the economic after-effects of September 11, 2001, were not as severe as anticipated, and there are grounds for cautious optimism about the years ahead. Certainly the West has shared in Canada's rapid rate of growth in recent quarters. Of course, predicting the West's economic future is not nearly as straightforward as predicting its demographic future. That said, current economic trends can help identify key opportunities and challenges for the region.

Continued GDP Growth

Over the past decades, western Canada's gross domestic product (GDP) has grown in both absolute and proportionate terms. As of 1999, the West accounted for 31 per cent of national GDP, slightly greater than the region's population weighting. Once again, however, significant differences exist within the region. Although the 1990s were a period of considerable GDP growth for the three prairie provinces, particularly when considered in per capita terms, Figure 5.10 shows that British Columbia's GDP barely kept pace with its population growth. By contrast, Saskatchewan and Alberta recorded real per capita growth in excess of 20 per cent.

FIGURE 5.10: REAL PER CAPITA GDP GROWTH IN THE 1990s

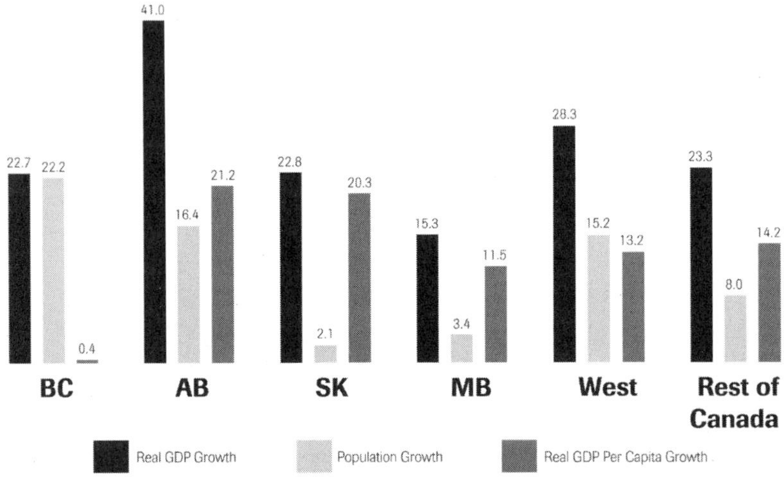

Source: Roach and Berdahl

What can explain the high GDP growth in Alberta and Saskatchewan and, to a lesser extent, Manitoba, over the 1990s? One contributing factor is the innovation that has improved industrial productivity, particularly the adoption of new technologies in agriculture and oil and gas. Another is the liberalization of global and particularly continental trade, which has opened up markets for western Canadian goods. Added to this was the impact of a weak Canadian dollar that made western exports more attractive to foreign markets and increased the earnings of Canadian exporters. There is reason to assume, moreover, that GDP growth will continue in the years ahead, particularly if the potential labour shortages noted in the previous section can be addressed. Industries continue to seek out ways to use new technologies to improve productivity and to lower costs, and agricultural producers continue to develop new niche markets in North America and abroad. If the American economy rebounds, American demand for western Canadian products should continue to grow in the years ahead. However, a potential fly in this ointment is the threat of American protectionism, a threat unlikely to be negated by NAFTA.

Growing Reliance on International Exports

As a producer of natural resources, western Canada has always been a trading region. What is new is that the West's trade in natural resources is increasingly heading towards international markets while interprovincial (internal) trade is shrinking in relative importance. Between 1981 and 1999, western Canada's international exports grew by 200 per cent. Over the same period, interprovincial trade grew by only 45 per cent. These dramatically different growth rates impact the region's international-internal trade ratio; as of 1999, roughly 60 per cent of the region's trade was destined for international markets, with the remaining 40 per cent headed to Canadian markets. Figure 5.11 provides detailed illustrations of the changing weights of international and interprovincial exports across the four western provinces. In British Columbia and Saskatchewan the gap has widened over the past 20 years, in Alberta it first opened up in 1992, and in Manitoba it may just be emerging. In all four cases, however, international trade has been increasing as a proportion of provincial GDP.

Although the growth in international trade is common across the four western provinces, they differ in the level of their dependence on American markets. "International trade" is a bit of a misnomer, as over 78 per cent of western Canada's international exports went to the United States in 2000. Alberta and Manitoba are the most dependent on

FIGURE 5.11: REAL INTERNATIONAL AND INTERPROVINCIAL
EXPORTS AS A PER CENT OF GDP, 1981-2000

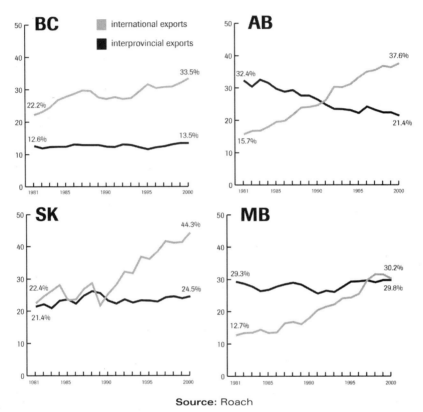

Source: Roach

American markets, with over 80 per cent (almost 90 per cent in Alberta's case) of international exports in both provinces destined for the United States in 2000. For Saskatchewan and British Columbia, over 60 per cent of exports in 2000 were destined for the American market.

This regional reliance on American markets, which is not out of line with the national pattern, has been largely positive. However, it does present at least two key risks. The first is that western Canada's economic fortunes rise and fall with the American economy: if it takes a significant downturn, the western Canadian economy will take the hit. There is no escaping regional, and for that matter national, vulnerability with respect to American markets. The second and closely related risk—indeed, reality—is that individual industries are vulnerable to swings in American public policy. Recent examples include the softwood lumber dispute — a Canada-US trade dispute that primarily affected British Columbia, which supplies 50 per cent of Canada's softwood lumber exports — and the 2002 increase in American agricultural subsidies. Since September 11, although perhaps coincidentally, we have seen growing protectionism in the United States, a movement that potentially affects a broad swath of western Canadian exports running from softwood lumber to beef, pork, and a range of agricultural products. Therefore, the West's growing reliance on American markets carries with it a growing vulnerability to protectionist measures in the United States, measures that it was hoped NAFTA would deter. To date, however, NAFTA's protection has been modest at best.

Despite what one may think by watching protesters at G8 summits and other international meetings, the general population sees global trade as benefiting their province and Canada as a whole.[12] Given that there is a limited internal market for western Canada's natural resource products, there is every reason to believe that international trade will continue to grow in importance for western Canada.

Slow But Continued Growth in Interprovincial Trade

While interprovincial trade has not grown at nearly the same rate as international trade, the fact remains that internal markets are still important to western Canada, accounting for $52.4 billion in goods and services in 1999. As noted in Chapter 1, much of western Canada's interprovincial trade is internal to the region itself, with almost 50 per cent being accounted for by trade with other western Canadian provinces. This points to an important inter-regional economy, and speaks to the need for reduced internal trade barriers and an efficient regional transportation system. Ideally, interprovincial barriers to trade will continue to fall across the country, but in the absence of concerted national action there may well be an opportunity to address trade barriers within the regional context alone. In this way, provincial governments in the West may lead the way to a reinvigorated national effort to eliminate interprovincial barriers to trade and the mobility of human capital.

Diversification But Continued Dependence on Resource Industries

Despite years of aspiring to diversify the regional economy, the West remains heavily dependent on the export of price-volatile resource and agricultural commodities. As Figure 5.12 illustrates, the western provinces vary in the specific character of their export resource dependency: wood and pulp and paper in British Columbia, oil and natural gas in Alberta, agricultural products and oil and gas in Saskatchewan. Only Manitoba has a diversified export profile that features a disproportionately greater reliance on manufactured products.

FIGURE 5.12: TOP FIVE EXPORTS BY INDUSTRY, 2000

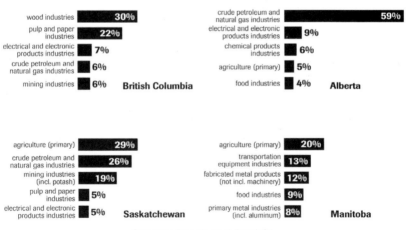

Source: Roach and Berdahl

Public Policy Implications of Economic Trends

These economic trends point to two large challenges for western Canada. The first is the need to ensure an efficient transportation infrastructure

— north-south and east-west trade corridors alike must be seen as critically important strategic investments. Unfortunately, this is a policy area where the West has been a relatively poor performer. The provincial transportation systems are not well integrated, and public funding for infrastructure has been inconsistent and, at times, episodic. The political fact is that, when push comes to shove, it is easier to cut funding for transportation infrastructure than it is to cut social spending. What is often not recognized, however, is that the tax dollars that pay for social spending are dependent on the health of the economy and that the regional economy is dependent on its transportation infrastructure. If the West is to be competitive in the years ahead, it is crucial that public policy debates begin to center on transportation issues, including discussions about alternative funding mechanisms such as public-private partnerships. The prosperity of the West depends upon a regional transportation system that can connect western producers to distant global markets. This was true in the past, is true today, and will still be true tomorrow.

The second challenge is the continued need for economic diversification. Governments must find ways to reduce disincentives to diversification and to create incentives. This is not to say that governments should start to pick "winners" and "losers," prop up non-viable industries, establish crown corporations, or become major actors in the economy. Far from it. At the same time, however, public policy has a role to play. Diversification is not an inevitable product of a market-based economy operating in a regional context.

Simply put, but not so simple to apply, there is a need to develop strategies to help build the new economy, a knowledge-based economy, in the New West. This will mean, in part, building from existing strengths and the existing resource base, by developing, for example, a petroleum consulting business that can compete across the world long after Alberta's conventional oil and natural gas resources are in decline. It may also mean building an agricultural bio-tech industry in Saskatchewan and Manitoba that is immune to seasonal variations in crops and a multi-media industry in British Columbia that can compete with the world's best.

Trends in the Public Sector

Identifying demographic trends is relatively easy, while identifying economic trends is somewhat more challenging. Identifying political trends moves us even further down the scale from science to art. While it is possible to identify the key trends on the horizon, unexpected political events can rapidly tip them in very different directions. This was seen historically with the North American social movements of the 1960s, the fall of the Berlin Wall, and, some suggest, the September 11 terrorist attacks on the United States. That said, planning must be done based on the best information available at the time; a lack of certainty is no excuse for a failure to plan strategically.

Challenges with Debt Repayment

Western Canada's dominant public policy debate of the 1990s was deficit elimination and debt repayment. On the first point, the three prairie provinces were largely successful — Alberta, Saskatchewan, and Manitoba each managed to balance their budgets in the 1990s, and, given public distaste for deficits, it is unlikely that these provinces will return to the large deficit spending patterns of the 1980s. In fact, both Alberta and Manitoba have legislated prohibitions relating to budgetary deficits. That said, it must be noted that projected government revenues in Alberta and Saskatchewan are influenced by volatile natural resource markets, placing continual strain on provincial budgeting. Saskatchewan in particular is being buffeted by drought and depressed agricultural markets.

Unlike its regional partners, British Columbia stood out by not addressing deficit issues in the 1990s. As Figure 5.13 shows, successive NDP governments not only failed to prioritize deficit elimination but ran up growing deficits, a pattern in sharp contrast to both NDP and Conservative governments on the prairies. This situation potentially changed with the 2001 election of the Liberal Party, which has publicly

FIGURE 5.13: PROVINCIAL GOVERNMENT SURPLUS/DEFICITS, 1994-2000

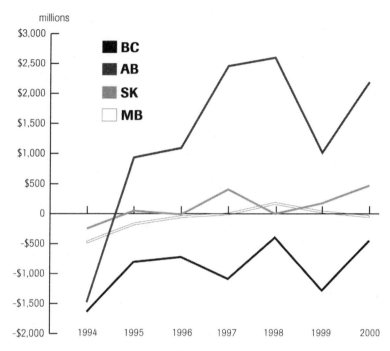

Source: Roach and Berdahl

committed to achieving a balanced budget by 2004-05. Its efforts to do so, and the programmatic costs associated with deficit reduction, will be some of the most closely watched public policy stories for the early 2000s. In the short term, moreover, deficit budgets will still prevail as the British Columbia provincial government tries to get its fiscal house in order in the face of soft export markets.

On the second dominant policy issue of the 1990s — debt elimination — western Canada has had much more modest success. Figure 5.14 presents the provincial debts for 1994 and 2000, calculated as a percentage of provincial GDP. As the figure shows, and as one should expect given its decade of deficits, British Columbia increased its total net tax-supported debt in both GDP and per capita terms. In other words, the absolute value of British Columbia's debt increased at a faster rate than did its GDP and its population. The three prairie provinces, however, had a very different experience. Alberta clearly stands out: the Alberta government under Ralph Klein made debt elimination a dominant theme, and the government's fiscal restraint, combined with high oil and gas prices, an expanding economy, and population growth, enabled the province to reduce its debt levels considerably. In per capita terms, Alberta's debt levels fell from $9,116 per Albertan in 1994 to $3,213 in 2000 — the lowest level in Canada.

FIGURE 5.14: TOTAL NET TAX-SUPPORTED DEBT, 1994 AND 2000

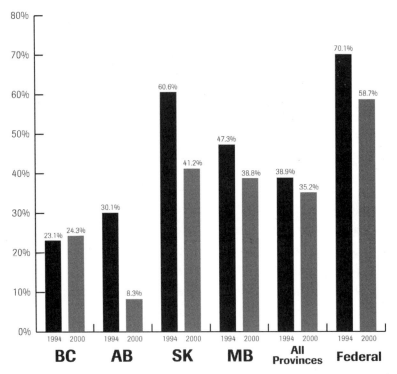

Source: Roach and Berdahl

With much less aggressive pursuit of debt elimination, and with lower resource revenues, economic expansion, and population growth, it is notable that Saskatchewan and Manitoba were also able to reduce their debt loads considerably between 1994 and 2000. Saskatchewan was the only province other than Alberta to reduce its absolute debt value, while Manitoba reduced its debt as a percentage of provincial GDP. However, because Saskatchewan and Manitoba debt levels were so high to begin with, both provinces still have a long way to go on the road to debt elimination. Even so, all provincial governments in the West are in a better debt position than is the federal government.

So, where does all of this leave us? Alberta is the only province within striking distance of debt elimination, and it is likely that the government will continue to maintain this as a policy goal. British Columbia, which, not incidentally, moved from being a "have" to a "have not" province in 2001, is now receiving federal equalization payments and is years away from deficit elimination, much less debt reduction. Saskatchewan and Manitoba have the potential to keep chipping away, bit by bit, at their debt levels, but as in all provincial administrations it is possible that other issues may emerge as more important to politicians and the electorate alike. This is particularly true given the demographic challenges noted in Saskatchewan and Manitoba, although the pressures exerted on provincial budgets by health care will not leave anyone untouched. (Hence the provincial chorus for a greater financial contribution from Ottawa.) Overall, it is likely that the policy importance of debt reduction, although not deficit elimination, will wane in the years ahead, as it has with the federal government.

Increased Political Role of Cities

As noted earlier, the urbanization trend means that more western Canadians live in cities than in rural areas. This is true even for the relatively rural province of Saskatchewan. What is notable in recent years is that municipal governments, particularly in the larger census metropolitan areas (CMAs), are becoming more aware of their political clout and more assertive in its use. Mayors across the West are increasingly vocal about their dissatisfaction with the status quo: the lack of adequate municipal powers, the issue of downloading and offloading from the provincial and federal governments, limited fiscal resources, and growing citizen demand for municipal services. This is seen in the participation of three western cities — Vancouver, Calgary, and Winnipeg — in the C5 initiative, which brings together the mayors of Canada's "hub cities" to promote their role in Canada's cultural, economic, and political life. Municipal associations, such as the Alberta Union of Municipal Associations, the Union of British Columbia Municipalities, and the Federation of Canadian Municipalities, are emerging as political actors. In short, there is a municipal revolution emerging in western Canada, and in Canada as a whole.

Increased political voice, of course, does not necessarily mean political clout or policy change; being heard is not the same thing as being taken into account. The large cities have a number of barriers to realizing change in their political status and policy autonomy. First, municipal governments are not constitutionally recognized, falling instead among the many responsibilities of the provincial governments. This need not be a barrier in and of itself,[13] but Canadian legislation and court decisions have resulted in a system that requires provincial governments to amend their legislation if growing urban aspirations are to be accommodated. The challenge, then, for the big cities is to have provincial governments recognize the value to the provincial economy that will come with empowering cities. Second, urban areas are under-represented in both federal and provincial legislative assemblies. The Supreme Court of Canada has ruled that electoral districts can vary in population size by up to plus or minus 25 per cent. The urban areas, as a result, have more heavily populated electoral ridings than do rural areas. This under-representation of urban areas undermines the voicing of urban concerns within provincial legislatures and the House of Commons. Third, there remains a challenge in creating a legislative system within the provinces that recognizes the particular needs of large cities. With a few exceptions (e.g., the Vancouver Act and the Winnipeg Act), municipal governments in western Canada are legislatively bound by provincial Municipal Acts — legislation that covers municipalities ranging from small villages and towns to large cities approaching populations of one million.[14] Provincial and municipal governments will need to work together to decide to what degree population differences need to be reflected in legislation, and how to accommodate such size variations.

The good news is that the provincial and federal governments are beginning to recognize this urban reality. In 2001-02, the Prime Minister's Caucus Task Force on Urban Issues focused a federal eye on urban issues, reconsidering the federal role in cities. The British Columbia government is actively working on community charter legislation that will potentially allow greater powers and/or autonomy to municipalities, and all the prairie governments are updating or have recently reviewed their municipal legislation.

How all of this will evolve is not clear. What is clear is that urban policy issues will emerge at the forefront of western Canadian policy debate with greater frequency and that western Canada's mayors and municipal associations will continue to participate vigorously in this debate. Debates about the future of the New West and about the determinants of regional prosperity will increasingly, although not exclusively, become policy debates about the urban West.

Growing Competition for Policy Space

The myriad demographic and economic trends, combined with the continued government desire to appear fiscally prudent, result in a rather packed policy space. Governments — federal, provincial, and municipal — are being asked to address a number of valid and pressing issues and to invest in health care, education, social services, urban infrastructure, transportation, environmental protection, the military, arts and culture, and the non-profit sector. They are expected to create a positive business environment through competitive tax rates and limited regulations and to keep public sector salaries for education, health care, and municipal employees competitive with the private sector. They are to reallocate resources to municipal and Aboriginal governments while protecting the environment and attracting immigrants. And, if there is anything left to spare, they are expected to pay down public debt. Even if governments had unlimited fiscal resources, balancing these many policy issues and directions would be challenging. Add to this the reality of limited fiscal resources, and governments more than ever are left in the position of making hard choices and balancing competing interests.

Policy space will grow more complex and competitive in the years ahead, and some policy issues, by their very nature, are less likely than others to attract public support and political momentum. Take, for example, the issue of providing a regional transportation infrastructure linking western Canadian producers to global markets. The ability of western Canadian businesses and industries to compete nationally and internationally is dependent on an efficient, well-integrated transportation system, one able to meet the growing needs of a region that remains, despite the information highway, physically distant from the centres of continental and global trade. The ability of governments to have a sufficient tax base from which to pay for programs such as health care and public education is dependent on the economy. By extension, then, the future of public programs is, in part, dependent on regional transportation systems. However, in policy debates, transportation issues receive very little consideration and are easy to cut in difficult fiscal times. Given the hard choice between freezing funding for education or health versus cutting funding for transportation, governments are naturally tempted to make the short-term political choice of cutting transportation funding.

Similar examples can be found in other fields. Because of this, different interest groups and organizations — unions, business associations, municipal associations — can be expected to grow increasingly vocal in the years ahead as they attempt to garner public support and awareness for their policy areas.

Continental Integration

North American integration has emerged as a hot topic in recent years, particularly after the implementation of NAFTA and the tragic events of September 11, 2001. Policy issues surrounding North American security have opened up larger debates about immigration policy, market access, and monetary policy (in particular, the abandonment of the Canadian dollar). Not surprisingly, continental integration debates lead naturally to debates about Canadian sovereignty. Will continental integration mean the loss of a truly distinct Canada? Will it undermine Canadian culture or nationally cherished programs such as publicly funded health care? Will Canada, the economically, politically, and demographically weaker of the partners, be able to fully protect its long-term interests?

Issues associated with continental integration are not only complex and extremely broad in scope, they also play out differently across the Canadian regions. This, of course, should not be surprising, for we witnessed the same effect in debates about the National Policy, reciprocity in the 1911 federal election, the National Energy Program, and the implementation of both the Free Trade Agreement in 1989 and NAFTA four years later. Given that patterns of Canadian-American trade, American direct investment, partisan support, and cultural industries all vary along regional lines, the debates about continental integration will inevitably become entangled with regional interests, conflicts, and values. The policy challenge for western Canadians and their governments is to ensure that regional interests and perspectives are fully reflected in national debates about continental integration.

Over the long term, the dynamics of continental integration raise questions about regional and provincial identities just as much as they raise questions about the national identity of Canadians, including those in the West. How will western Canadians come to see their region and province within the context of greater continental integration? Will integration present opportunities for sustaining regional prosperity, for building a quality of life that could be the envy of the world? Or—

perhaps and/or—might greater integration weaken the sense of regional and even provincial community as individuals redirect their lives to continental challenges, opportunities, and aspirations?

Increased Aboriginal Political Assertiveness

It is not surprising that Aboriginal policy issues will form a considerable and quite likely growing part of western Canada's policy agenda in the years ahead. Policy-makers and the general public must anticipate that the Aboriginal community — through individual Aboriginal leaders as well as numerous provincial and national organizations — will demand that their voices be heard in any policy field that directly concerns their people. Aboriginal leaders arc increasingly demanding consultation and engagement; simply put, after over a century of public policy that undermined their interests and well-being, many Aboriginal people do not trust government policies to protect their interests.

One challenge with this is the lack of a single voice for Aboriginal people in western Canada (or in Canada, for that matter). In some cases, particularly in the case of reserves, Aboriginal peoples speak with a clear and emphatic voice. In other cases, particularly within urban centres where the majority of the Aboriginal population in western Canada now resides, an effective Aboriginal political voice is often absent. This reality can make consultation, from the government's perspective, a time-consuming and frustrating process. However, given the high level of distrust that has developed, this frustration may simply be something that governments will need to bear.

There is nothing neat or easy about the Aboriginal policy agenda. The distrust goes back for generations, with the legacy of colonialism, highly stressed Aboriginal communities, racism in the larger society, and individuals who do not enjoy a level of material comfort and personal well-being comparable to that enjoyed by other Canadians. The policy process is complex, cumbersome, and conflictual, and the policy remedies contentious, costly, and uncertain. Indeed, all we know for certain is that if Aboriginal policy issues are not addressed with greater vigor and success, regional prosperity for all western Canadians will be imperiled.

Conflict Between Economic and Environmental Goals

The balance between economic prosperity and environmental protection has never been an easy one, and this balance will be brought into question more frequently in the years ahead. Finding a balance, ensuring that the quest for prosperity today does not damage the environmental legacy for generations tomorrow, is a particularly difficult issue for western Canada, given its economic reliance on natural resources. This issue was brought into focus in western Canada in 2002 by acrimonious debates about the implementation of the Kyoto Accord. As Canada moves to address its international environmental commitments and goals, careful attention will need to be paid to regional economic effects. Left ignored, these effects could reinvigorate western alienation.

In the years to come, the environmental agenda will only expand. Climate change, water and air quality, water supply in the face of drought and urban growth on the prairies, sustainable forestry, and endangered species are just some of the issues that will generate political debate and conflict. As western Canadians and their governments turn to address this complex and difficult agenda, it will be important to find ways to reconcile environmental protection and economic prosperity.

Strategic Directions for the West

Taken together, where do these demographic, economic, and political trends point? Can strategic directions be identified for western Canada as a regional community? Can we reach beyond the specific policy concerns addressed above? Five key priorities can be identified that must be strategically addressed in the interests of long-term regional prosperity.[15]

1. *The West must create the tools to attract, retain, and build human capital.*
   As the demographic trends outlined in this chapter have indicated,
   the West faces a serious challenge in the years ahead in terms of
   labour supply and tax base. Public policies are needed to increase
   the number of immigrants coming to and remaining in western
   Canada, to increase Aboriginal engagement in the regional economy, and to attract and retain the young skilled workers who are so
   integral to the new knowledge-based economy. Policies are also
   needed to ensure that western Canada's postsecondary system —
   including universities, colleges, trade institutions, and apprentice-
   ship programs — meets the future training needs of the region.
   Taken together, these facts speak to the need for a strategic
   approach to the development of human capital, one that mobilizes
   the resources of both the federal and provincial governments and
   one that is regional in scope.

2. *The West must continue economic diversification.* Economic diversification continues to be a challenge for the region. While advances
   have been made, the opportunities for adding value to natural
   resources, rather than exporting raw materials to be processed
   elsewhere, have not been fully tapped. The West also has an
   opportunity to expand its "new economy" industries in such fields
   as biotechnology, medical research, aerospace, and alternative
   energy sources. Making this transition will require a globally
   competitive region, defined by a positive business environment (in
   terms of regulation and tax rates); a high quality of life; and a large,
   diversified, and skilled labour force. This in turn means that public
   policy choices will shape the conditions for regional competitiveness and economic diversification.

3. *The West must strengthen its transportation infrastructure.* Western
   Canada's transportation infrastructure — its highways, railways,
   airports, pipelines, and ports — provides the foundation of the
   regional economy. Even e-commerce and service industries are
   dependent on transportation to move their goods — or, at the very

least, to supply the computers upon which their commerce is based. As a sparsely populated, extremely large land mass located at the geographic margins of the national and continental economies, western Canada is highly dependent on its transportation network. If the region's goods do not move efficiently, it adds costs to producers, costs that are ultimately passed on to consumers, thus making the West's goods less competitive. Failing to invest appropriately in our transportation network damages long-term competitiveness.

4. *The West must promote the global competitiveness of its major cities.* As this chapter noted, western Canada is increasingly an urban region, and cities are widely acknowledged as the primary drivers of growth in the new economy. The major urban regions are the West's, as well as some of Canada's, major gateways to the global economy. Without an effective urban strategy, one that addresses the quality of life in the large cities, western Canada will not be able to fully meet its economic potential.

5. *The West must develop new ways of facilitating regional coordination.* The four western provinces face common challenges that demand a degree of regional coordination if they are to be successfully addressed. Working together allows the provinces to find regional efficiencies. However, western Canadians lack the institutional capacity to plan regionally. For this reason, the cooperation and coordination so essential for regional prosperity cannot be fostered without significant institutional development.

Although these five priorities do not encompass the totality of policy concerns confronting western Canadians and their governments, they do provide an important start for those seeking to ensure economic prosperity within an increasingly competitive and challenging global economy. If western Canadians do not get these fundamentals right, it will be difficult to pursue other policy objectives. There must be a strong regional foundation on which prosperous and caring provincial communities can be built.

These priorities naturally lead to another question: whose responsibility are they? Should the federal government take the lead on these issues, or provincial governments, or municipal governments? This chapter has shown that demographic, economic, and political trends within the West tend to be highly interdependent. This points in turn to the inevitability of policy interdependence and the need for a system of governance that is able to accommodate rather than frustrate policy interdependence.

Notes

[1] Cited in Roger Gibbins, *Building the New West: A Framework for Regional Prosperity* (Calgary, AB: Canada West Foundation, 2001).

[2] In recent years, Ontario and Alberta have been the clear winners in the inter-provincial mobility sweepstakes.

[3] Mordecai Richler, "Stop complaining about the brain drain: Jesse Helms may clue into Canada's cultural imperialism," *National Post* 21 August 1999.

[4] As Canadian fertility rates have been falling, American rates have stabilized at a significantly higher level (2.08 in 1999). Kim Lunman, "Canada losing to US in baby race," *Globe and Mail* 4 July 2002: A9.

[5] Government of Singapore (n.d.). Baby Bonus Scheme System website, <http://www.babybonus.gov.sg>.

[6] In raw terms, Canada accepts more skilled individuals through immigration than we lose through the brain drain to the United States; thus, the net "brain drain" appears to work to our advantage. However, a great deal depends on how effectively immigrants are integrated into the Canadian economy. If immigrants find employment in jobs that fail to capitalize on their education, then the fact that we are gaining as many PhDs through immigration as we are losing through the brain drain can be very misleading.

[7] *Pioneers 2000* was held in Winnipeg in May, 2000, and was hosted by the Business Council of Manitoba, the Canada West Foundation, and the Council for Canadian Unity.

[8] Mary Jane Norris, Don Kerr, and Francois Nault, "Projections of the Population with Aboriginal Identity in Canada, 1991-2016," Royal Commission on Aboriginal Peoples, 1995.

[9] Manitoba Bureau of Statistics, *Manitoba's Aboriginal Populations Projected 1991- 2016.* This is a study prepared for the Native Affairs Secretariat, Manitoba Northern Affairs, 1997.

[10] At present, and despite public misperceptions, Aboriginal people living off reserve are subject to taxation. This may change for registered Indians in years ahead with court challenges, but it is unlikely to change for non-registered Indians and the Metis.

[11] Robert Roach and Loleen Berdahl, *State of the West: Western Canadian Demographic and Economic Trends* (Calgary, AB: Canada West Foundation, 2001). The 2001 Census data on Aboriginal labour market participation and employment levels were not publicly available at the time of writing.

[12] In the 2001 *Looking West* survey, 58.9 per cent of regional respondents agreed that "increased global trade has been good for Canada," and 57.5 per cent agreed that it has been good for their province. The most negative provincial assessments came from respondents in British Columbia and Saskatchewan. Berdahl 18.

[13] Loleen Berdahl and Sophie Sapergia, *Urban Nation, Federal State* (Calgary, AB: Canada West Foundation, 2001).

14 Saskatchewan's new Cities Act covers the province's 13 largest cities, which still vary greatly in size.

15 These recommendation flow from a year-long consultation process that included public sessions in Edmonton, Saskatoon, Vancouver, and Winnipeg (the four brought together almost 400 community leaders); extensive opinion polling; demographic research; and a day-long round-table featuring Allan Blakeney, Gary Filmon, Michael Harcourt, Peter Lougheed, and Preston Manning.

CHAPTER 6

REGIONAL GOVERNANCE IN AN INTERDEPENDENT WORLD

"There are two very different visions of Canada being put
forward today.... One vision of Canada is that we are too small
and weak to prosper unless we are fully controlled at the centre,
of course, being Ottawa.... There is another vision of Canada.
This vision recognizes that the prosperity in one region is bene-
ficial to all regions. It is a vision of Canada where bitterness, frustration and confrontation are replaced by an awareness that there
has to be equity, there has to be fairness between the regions,
wherever you live in Canada and whatever the colour of your
political map.... It is clearly my personal vision."[1]

—PETER LOUGHEED, former Premier of Alberta.

Introduction

To this point we have discussed the enduring problems of western alienation and have considered potential strategies through which the federal
and provincial governments might address both alienation and regional
aspirations. We have also discussed the emerging public policy agenda
in western Canada and the extent to which policy challenges have been
made more acute by changes in the global environment. It is this interplay between regional discontent and a globally infused policy agenda
that will provide much of the pith and substance for western Canadian

176

politics in the years to come. Given, furthermore, the reciprocal relationship between regional and national prosperity, we called for the active engagement of all governments in the West in addressing the dilemma of western alienation and the host of related public policy challenges. The underlying tone in the analysis has been optimistic, albeit tempered by the concern that ongoing problems will be left to fester, thus imperiling the prospects for regional prosperity within an increasingly competitive global environment.

The discussion so far, however, has focused largely on what governments can do *on their own*. It is now time to recognize that the public policy landscape in Canada — and for that matter the policy landscape around the world — at the start of the twenty-first century is shaped by the realities of *policy interdependence* and *multi-level governance*. It is, therefore, essential to turn to these new realities in the context of western Canada and to explore how governments might work together to address regional challenges and aspirations.

The Case for Policy Interdependence and Multi-Level Governance

Governments no longer act in splendid isolation, if they ever did. Although the United States, the world's one remaining superpower, may at times be a troubling exception, it is the exception that proves the rule. Governments in Canada are not exceptions. Their actions impinge on other governments, both domestic and foreign, and are in turn constrained by the actions of other governments. Policy decisions taken by one government inevitably ripple through, or come splashing through, the policy domains of others. Regional trade agreements such as NAFTA and international frameworks such as the WTO further constrain the actions of national and sub-national governments. Given, then, the growing inability to act effectively alone, governments across the board are developing new ways to work together. In this instance, necessity is indeed the mother of invention.

A few examples can be used to illustrate the new public policy landscape characterized by multi-level governance and policy interdependence:

1. The Canadian health care system provides a graphic illustration of policy interdependence and multi-level governance. While the federal government's actions with respect to the Canada Health Act, funding for medical research, and fiscal transfers to the provinces are important parts of the larger puzzle, even more so are the policy frameworks and financial decisions of provincial governments. Nor are local authorities left out of the picture. The population health policies needed to create and sustain "healthy cities" fall partially within the jurisdiction of local governments, and some municipal authorities provide medical services such as ambulances. Regional health authorities in provinces across the West, even though not yet full-fledged governments, are increasingly making a range of decisions bearing directly on health care delivery and priorities. In addition, First Nations governments come into play, as does the international environment when health care providers based outside the country begin to enter the Canadian market. The growing availability of medical information, advice, and even pharmaceuticals over the Internet adds on layers of additional complications. If there are solutions to a looming health care crisis, they are not to be found in the policies of any one government acting alone.

2. Over the last decade, First Nations governments have assumed more and more control over the policy environment of their communities. These governments, however, are inherently limited in terms of their practical policy autonomy. The limitation springs not from constitutional restrictions per se but rather from the human resource base of most First Nations, where resident adult populations in the hundreds rather than the thousands are the norm. Policy matters such as postsecondary education, emergency medical services, advanced medical care, and transportation infra-

structure must necessarily be handled through multi-level governance. Aboriginal communities are unavoidably embedded within
the policy frameworks of the encompassing provincial and national
communities.

3.   The tax and regulatory policies pursued by individual provinces
ripple out across the federation. In part, this is by design. For
example, Alberta's low tax strategy, "The Alberta Advantage," is
intended to lure financial investment and human capital from
other provinces and even other countries. Competing governments are forced to respond, and in some cases the competition is
welcomed; recent Ontario governments have played the tax
competition game with considerable enthusiasm. However,
Alberta's western Canadian neighbours are less able to handle the
downward pressure on tax revenues.[2] The situation gets worse if
relatively wealthy governments reach public-sector wage settle-
ments that drive wages up in neighbouring provinces at the same
time that tax revenues are being eroded. Nonetheless, failure to
compete on either the tax or salary front will lead to the flight of
human capital.

4.   The recent national debate over the ratification of the Kyoto
Accord on climate change provides an excellent if somewhat inco-
herent illustration of policy interdependence. The climate change
objectives endorsed by the federal government cannot be achieved
without the active collaboration of provincial and municipal
governments, and, not surprisingly, those same governments have
sought input into federal policy.

For western Canadians, poised on the cusp of a new century, regional
prosperity will rest on the effective management of policy interdependence and multi-level governance. Now, not surprisingly, the mention of
multi-level governance tends to direct our attention to relationships
moving up and down the political food chain: federal-provincial, provin-
cial-municipal, federal-municipal, and even national-international and

provincial-international relations. The term "level" inadvertently and unfortunately reinforces hierarchical perceptions of government and intergovernmentalism. (As a consequence, provincial governments adamantly reject the phrase "levels of government" and opt instead for "orders of government"; big city governments are also fastening onto the phrase "order of government" to describe their own standing.) It is essential, however, not to neglect *horizontal* policy interaction. For this reason, our discussion of multi-level governance begins with an examination of interprovincial cooperation within the context of western Canada before moving on to more conventional federal-provincial relationships and to the institutional framework within which those latter relationships take place. The discussion of the potential for institutional reform is then broadened to consider the place of cities within the context of multi-level governance and policy interdependence. Finally, we turn to strategic partnerships that might be forged between western Canada and other regional communities within both Canada and the United States.

Our interest throughout lies with the interplay of governments and their respective communities within the western Canadian policy environment. Traditionally, this interplay has been associated with intergovernmental acrimony and conflict; it is the political arena that most often dismays Canadians as their governments appear to fight, like the gladiators of old, rather than cooperate. Not coincidentally, it is the arena where western alienation has contributed heavily to both the stage settings and the script. However, if our understanding of increasing policy interdependence is correct, it is also the arena within which many regional challenges will be addressed and, with luck, regional aspirations realized.

Interprovincial Cooperation

The discussion in the preceding chapters has raised a slew of policy issues that cannot be bottled up within provincial boundaries or, for that matter, within the jurisdictional boundaries of governments. Transportation connections to the global economy do not start and end at provincial boundaries; the Port of Vancouver, perched on the edge of the Pacific Ocean, is the terminus for not only a regional but also the national transportation system that snakes for thousands of kilometers back into the interior of the continent. Environmental effects are oblivious to political lines on the map, and western Canadians function within a labour market that is regional and national as much as it is provincial. Individuals may go to school in one province, work in another, and perhaps retire in yet another. Power grids potentially span the region, and common waterways cross the prairie provinces. In effect, there is a great deal of spillover across provincial and jurisdictional boundaries.

One conceptual approach for handling such spillovers is to assign legislative responsibility for issues that cross provincial boundaries to the national government. Ottawa, for example, could pick up responsibility for the regional transportation system, given that road and rail links do not end at provincial boundaries, and for manpower training (including postsecondary education), given the mobility of the Canadian labour force. In a similar fashion, responsibility for environmental protection could be lodged with the national government. This approach, however, would result in a massive migration of powers and responsibilities to Ottawa, as there are very few policy areas than can be neatly contained as unique within provincial boundaries. Most policy areas have, at least to some degree, provincial and national dimensions. Moreover, relying upon Ottawa to address regional policy issues is a strategy that is incompatible with the lessons of western alienation. Western Canadians are unlikely to entrust the national government with an expanded policy mandate without first being assured of greater influence within and equitable treatment from that government. It would entail paying proportionately more taxes to a national government that is not trusted and beyond the control of the regional electorate and less to provincial governments lying within regional control. In short, as discussed in Chapter 5, a more centralized federal system makes no sense for western Canadians *unless it is accompanied by fundamental institutional reform* (more on this shortly).

If there is not a tidy single-government solution to regional policy issues, then we must explore interprovincial cooperation as a means to address those issues that spill across provincial boundaries. Here, there are certainly many incentives for greater interprovincial cooperation with respect to public policy and programs. First, it potentially provides a way of handling economy of scale problems that confront a small population — less than a third of the population of California — spread over a large and imposing landmass. For example, the regionally mandated and funded veterinarian college that the western provinces established at the University of Saskatchewan makes sense; there is insufficient demand to support four provincial colleges. Similar opportunities may well arise with medical services and university research. In the latter case, "centres of excellence" sprinkled across western Canadian universities (albeit largely funded through federal grants) promote and indeed mandate regional cooperation within the research community. Second, a seamless transportation system makes sense for virtually all aspects of the regional economy, and this can only be achieved through the lubricant of interprovincial cooperation. Third, regional cooperation may enhance the opportunities for labour force training and facilitate a better fit between human resources and employment opportunities. Along these lines, social work academics in Manitoba, Saskatchewan, and Alberta have come together to form the Prairie Child Welfare Consortium (PCWC) whose mission is to "build capacity, at different levels of all systems that support children, families and communities in the prairie provinces, while ensuring respect for the inherent right of Aboriginal self-government in child welfare."[3] More generally, interprovincial cooperation across the region may lead to improved program efficiencies and more cost-effective government. In this context it should be noted that web-based e-government provides the means to knit together provincial programming or, at the very least, to expose regional residents to a host of inter-connected program opportunities.

REGIONAL COOPERATION WITH SUPERCOMPUTERS

A new network of supercomputers, WestGrid, will link more than 250 researchers in Alberta and British Columbia who are working on projects dealing with atomic reactions, genomics, chemical reactions, space weather, long-range climate studies, the human genome project, and oil and gas exploration. WestGrid is a joint venture among Simon Fraser University, the New Media Innovation Centre, the Banff Centre, TRIUMF (Canada's national laboratory for particle and nuclear physics), and the Universities of Alberta, Calgary, and Lethbridge. It will enable researchers in the two western provinces to compete with the world's best and will hopefully draw scientific talent to the West.[4]

At the same time, there are clear constraints on the degree of cooperation that can be expected. In some important ways, the western provinces are in competition for interprovincial migrants, international immigrants, and new business. It would be unreasonable to expect such competition to abate completely, and, in fact, the regional and national economies might be less innovative and efficient without it. Intergovernmental competition likely strengthens the regional economy while at the same time it promotes pubic policy innovation and creativity. There are also important issues of accountability. It is one thing, for example, if an Edmonton resident contributes as a *federal* taxpayer to improvements to the transportation system in Saskatchewan. It is something quite different if she contributes as a *provincial* taxpayer through expenditure decisions taken by the Government of Alberta.

What is perhaps less clear in all of this is whether there is a need for a more formalized structure to intergovernmental relations among the four provinces, one that reaches beyond ad hoc program collaboration. Taken together, the four western Canadian provinces constitute more than an abstract geographical entity or a source of political identification. They also constitute a regional framework for intergovernmental relations, as do the Maritimes and, when Newfoundland and Labrador are included, the Atlantic provinces. Although this policy framework is not used as frequently as the more general framework provided by federal-provincial relations, it is still worthy of note.

The existing pattern of intergovernmental relations is most apparent in the relationship among the western premiers, who have worked together on a number of fronts. In 1965, Alberta, Saskatchewan, and Manitoba formed the Prairie Economic Council, which was expanded in 1973 to include British Columbia and renamed the Western Premiers' Conference (WPC). The WPC brought the four premiers together in advance of the 1973 Western Economic Opportunity Conference (WEOC) in Calgary; it is now an annual event preceded by a fair degree of intergovernmental consultation. It is complemented by growing ministerial and public-service interaction among the four provincial governments, only some of which is sparked by or flows through the WPC. (Most ministerial meetings, however, are still national rather than regional in scope.) The premiers' meetings have provided a way to amplify the West's regional voice, the assumption being that four provincial governments speaking in unison carry more weight with Ottawa and other premiers than do individual governments speaking alone. This strategy has been particularly useful in past constitutional debates, and its contemporary relevance is illustrated by the parallel strategies adopted by the big city mayors as they try to articulate and promote a common urban agenda.

To date, however, the WPC has not resulted in regional *governance*, by which we mean regional programs or policy initiatives jointly administered and funded by the four provincial governments. Although a few innovative steps have been taken, including the joint funding of the veterinary program, the WPC has been used primarily to coordinate criticisms of the federal government and, less commonly, to develop a common regional position for the Annual Premiers' Conference. WPC communiqués provide a useful itemization of regional grievances with respect to Ottawa, but offer much thinner gruel with respect to common action on the part of the provincial governments. The WPC's essential role is political rather than administrative or governance. It serves to strengthen personal relationships among the premiers and territorial leaders, and many of its activities, including golf, are directed to this end. Those personal relationships can, in turn, provide the foundation upon which more institutionalized relationships might be built, but to this point construction activity has been modest.

The question, then, is whether the four western provinces should move towards a more formalized and expansive network of intergovernmental relations. Here, we should note that the WPC has a design feature that complicates and may even preclude any evolution towards regional governance. In recent years, it has brought together not only the premiers of British Columbia, Alberta, Saskatchewan, and Manitoba, but also the territorial leaders of Nunavut, the Yukon, and the Northwest Territories. (Although Nunavut cannot be considered a part of western Canada by any stretch of the imagination, there is no other intergovernmental forum that would provide a logical home for its territorial leader.) As a result, three of the seven participants at the table represent in total only 1 per cent of the "regional" population; the *combined* population of the three northern territories is only 9 per cent of the smallest western province, Saskatchewan. The territorial governments also have a distinct northern agenda and a very different relationship with the Government of Canada. The northern territories are, in effect, financial wards of the federal government; financial transfers from Ottawa are an order of magnitude larger than those flowing from Ottawa to provincial governments in the West.

ADDRESSING THE EAST/WEST DIVIDE WITHIN THE WEST

An important test for the policy capacity of both interprovincial and federal-provincial relations will come from the growing demographic and economic divide between Manitoba and Saskatchewan, on the one side, and Alberta and British Columbia, on the other. As previous chapters have illustrated, this divide is manifested across a broad range of policy-related

issues: population growth, urbanization, economic prosperity, interprovincial migration, and the attraction of international immigrants. As a
consequence, it opens up a number of critically important questions.
Should the divide be addressed as a matter of public policy, or should
governments focus on the well-being of individual Canadians rather than
provincial communities? If the divide should be addressed, should it be
addressed through interprovincial cooperation or through federal
programs? Should Ottawa try to do for Manitoba and Saskatchewan what
it has tried (unsuccessfully) to do for Atlantic Canada over the past 50
years? Should we rely on markets to make the interprovincial adjustments?

Although it may be difficult to come to grips with these macro-questions,
our implicit answers to them will frame the way in which we address more
specific policy issues. Our answers may also frame how we address other
cleavages within the region, including those between the Aboriginal and
non-Aboriginal communities and between the urban and rural Wests.

Thus, the WPC collapses two regions, the West and the North, into
a single intergovernmental vehicle, and the opportunities for common
interests, much less joint action, are thereby reduced. If the WPC is to
evolve into a vehicle for regional program development and policy
coordination, if not integration, then a number of issues need to be
addressed. First, a way will have to be found to partition the provincial
and territorial governments, at least for some purposes. Although there
may be times when it makes sense to create a bridge between the western and northern agendas, at other times the two can best be addressed
in isolation. Second, the WPC will need some ongoing secretariat,
some institutional capacity and continuity beyond that provided by
rotating host governments. Third, the premiers will have to abandon
their preference for conference sites in small communities — the 2002
WPC was held in the Yukon's Dawson City — and convene instead in
the region's urban heartland where media and public exposure can be
maximized. Failure to take these steps will not marginalize the WPC
but will constrain the potential role that the WPC could play as a
regional voice and policy vehicle.

On balance, there is a convincing argument to be made for greater interprovincial cooperation and for the formalization of that cooperation through the growth of the WPC. There are two basic drivers. First, there may well be things that the region can do together that individual provinces cannot achieve. One example is the creation of an effective transportation grid that links western Canadian producers to world markets. Lying behind this driver is a basic demographic reality: the western Canadian provinces alone, and for that matter the region as a whole, have a small population base by world or even continental standards. The second driver is the realization that what cannot be accomplished through cooperation may have to be accomplished, if it is accomplished at all, through the federal government. Here, the legacy and ongoing dynamics of western alienation make this a less favoured option. Relying on Ottawa to address regional concerns in the West is a high risk strategy at best.

At the same time, there are very real limits to the potential for interprovincial cooperation. The provinces are competitors for human capital and economic investment, and provincial governments are accountable to provincial taxpayers who often lack a regional policy perspective. In short, while interprovincial cooperation has merits that should be pursued, it remains a complement to rather than an alternative to the active engagement of the Government of Canada. This conclusion also suggests that greater regional cooperation is not, at this point, a prelude to some more formal political union. Admittedly, the idea of a single prairie province, first endorsed by Frederick Haultain, has had some enduring currency. It was tackled in a 1970 conference in Lethbridge,[5] and the idea of a broader western Canadian political union has been advanced more recently by Ric Dolphin, Western Bureau Chief for Southam Press:

> I believe there is a collective western identity and that it clashes with the eastern one. I believe that Haultain's [single prairie province] idea was a good one. And I believe that the west, or at least a good portion of it, can be better served by joining together as a single powerful unit against Ottawa.[6]

For now, however, incremental steps towards greater regional coordination and cooperation should be seen as just that: incremental steps towards greater regional coordination and cooperation. Many of those steps, moreover, may come from outside government as the business, professional, and not-for-profit sectors try to realize the potential gains from regional cooperation and reduce the economy of scale costs associated with relatively small provincial communities.

Federal-Provincial Cooperation

Although interprovincial cooperation within the West is likely to be increasingly important for public policy in the years ahead, it is unlikely that such cooperation will come even close to supplanting the need for active federal government involvement in the region's policy agenda. The constraints on interprovincial competition, provincial differences in policy capacity, and the logic of using senior levels of government to address spillover effects all argue for a continuing federal role. At issue, then, is the nature of that role and whether it will be pursued through unilateral initiatives or through programmatic collaboration with provincial governments in the West.

WESTERN ECONOMIC OPPORTUNITIES CONFERENCE

In the 1972 general election the federal Liberals were reduced to a minority government, in large part due to the drubbing the party received at the hands of the western Canadian electorate. As a response to the surge in western alienation and to demonstrate the government's sensitivity to western Canadian issues, Prime Minister Pierre Trudeau convened the 1973 Western Economic Opportunities Conference in Calgary. To the surprise of the federal government representatives, the western premiers presented a united front despite marked partisan and ideological differences among their provinces. (Three of the premiers were New Democrats, and the fourth, Peter Lougheed, was a Progressive

Conservative.) The provincial premiers dominated the agenda, and, from the perspective of the federal government, WEOC could only be considered a failure. Former Alberta Premier Don Getty, who was then a minister in Lougheed's Alberta delegation, recalls Trudeau's reaction: "At the end of the second day, I can still see him reaching forward with the gavel and hitting the wooden block and saying, 'And so ends the first and only and last Western Opportunities Conference,' and then he just let the gavel fall."[7] Trudeau was prescient; over the last 30 years there has been no attempt by the federal government or, for that matter, the provincial premiers to resurrect WEOC.

The regional critique of Canadian political life developed in Chapter 2 strongly suggests that unilateral initiatives by the federal government, by which we mean stand-alone federal programs framed and funded without the active engagement of provincial governments, are unlikely to be a satisfactory tool for addressing regional concerns and aspirations. First, history teaches us that any such initiatives are likely to emerge from governments whose persistent preoccupation will be with other regions. Moreover, as the last chapter discussed in the context of Western Economic Diversification Canada, there is little appetite in the region for the types of economic development programs used unsuccessfully for decades in Atlantic Canada. History also teaches us that universal programs, for instance a new national transportation policy, are likely to impose disproportionately high costs on western Canadian taxpayers while delivering disproportionately low benefits. In effect, national programs tend to have a redistributive element that works systematically against the West.

All this suggests that the Government of Canada is at best an uncertain asset when it comes to addressing the West's policy priorities. At the same time, however, there is certainly room for collaborative programs with provincial governments in the West. The critical issue may well be the spirit of collaboration. Here, we have seen some positive straws in the wind. The 1998 Social Union Framework Agreement (SUFA), for example, was meant to signal a new collaborative spirit in federal-provincial relations, although hard evidence to this effect has been hard to find. The most promising development so far has been Ottawa's agreement to a dispute settlement mechanism to handle conflicting interpretations of the Canada Health Act, although even here Ottawa is determined not to be bound by recommendations from this mechanism.

What we must avoid is the easy assumption that the new world of policy interdependence means that provincial and municipal policies necessarily, or should, get rolled into national policy frameworks fashioned by the federal government. The recognition of policy interdependence must not be confused with the implicit or explicit acceptance of a policy or institutional hierarchy. Acknowledging the reality of multi-level governance is not an argument that decision-making power should drift upwards. If anything, it is likely the reverse, particularly when we bring large urban governments into the picture. More fundamentally, if the West is not well-served by provincial governments operating out of sync with the federal government — the "firewall strategy" discussed in Chapter 5 — unilateral policy action by the federal government is equally inappropriate.

POLICY INTERDEPENDENCE AND FEDERALISM

Federal systems of government are all about policy interdependence and multi-level governance; federal constitutions establish multi-level governance, define the powers of the respective orders of government, and, to a degree, provide a framework for handling policy interdependence. We might expect, therefore, that Canadians should be well-equipped by their federal institutions for the new policy environment. Unfortunately, we bring to this environment a badly dated understanding of federalism, which tends to emphasize autonomy rather than interdependence; we see this in discussions about sovereignty-association, the Alberta "firewall," and federal intrusions into provincial areas of jurisdiction. All governments, including the federal government, too often place greater value on protecting the capacity for autonomous action than on building the capacity for policy collaboration. We also have federal institutions that were poorly designed for the nineteenth century much less the twenty-first. Here, the Senate is an obvious example, but additional note should be made of the lack of any institutional connection between the Government of Canada and the major metropolitan centres. The integration of First Nations governments into the intergovernmental structures of the Canadian federal state and, more generally, the accommodation of Aboriginal peoples into the principles and institutions of Canadian federalism provide further examples of institutional deficiencies. Federalism as it presently exists does not equip us well for new global realities. In principle, federalism is the right approach, but the Canadian model of federalism is not the pick of the litter.

Not surprisingly, the discussion of federal-provincial collaboration takes us back to institutional reform, the longstanding bugbear of western Canadian politics. Collaborative agreements between the federal and provincial governments would be much easier to contemplate and construct if western Canadians had faith in both parties. However, as long as the federal government is viewed with suspicion, progress is likely to be slow and halting. It is appropriate, therefore, to return briefly to this most central of western Canadian political themes.

Institutional Reform

If the Government of Canada is to function effectively in an environment of multi-level governance and policy interdependence, it needs political and institutional sensitivity to regional, provincial, and municipal interests. The existing government is ill-equipped in this respect, and the shortcomings are multitudinous: an antiquated Senate shorn of any legitimacy as a regional chamber, the lack of a cabinet or bureaucratic interface with municipal governments, regionally unbalanced political parties, party discipline that inhibits the expression of regional interests, and a parliamentary system that increasingly concentrates political power in the hands of the prime minister. In short, the federal government is not prepared for the new governance environment; it lacks the institutional dexterity and agility that federalism should instill. Any discussion of regional prosperity in an interdependent world, therefore, inevitably loops back to the thorny issue of institutional reform. Certainly this is the case in western Canada where a lack of confidence in the neutrality of the federal government continually threatens to derail effective multi-level governance. It is difficult to move ahead when confidence in both parties is absent.

INTERSTATE AND INTRASTATE FEDERALISM

Political scientists draw a useful distinction between *interstate* and *intrastate* federalism, terms that refer to different ways in which provincial residents connect to their federal government. Interstate representation refers to indirect methods of representation that take place through provincial governments. A resident of Saskatoon, for example, may count on the Saskatchewan government to represent, advance, and protect her interests through the intergovernmental forums in which the Government of Saskatchewan participates. (Interstate federalism can also refer to the constitutional division of powers, which can shield provincial residents from the actions of the national government, but this meaning is less relevant here.) In other words, she channels her representation through the provincial government, which speaks on her behalf and can be held accountable for so doing. In the future, cities such as Saskatoon may also play a role in this respect. Intrastate representation refers to representation that takes place directly through federal politicians rather than indirectly through provincial (or municipal) politicians. MPs and Senators are the primary routes for intrastate federalism. Most of the institutional reform debate in western Canada focuses on the inadequacies of intrastate federalism — on the failure of MPs, Senators, and cabinet representatives to provide effective and transparent channels for regional representation.

Western Canadian discussions of institutional reform generally start, and unfortunately often end, with Senate reform. How do we explain this fixation? Why not tackle the dominant parliamentary institution, the House of Commons? Why not concentrate on party discipline within the House, on the closed nature of decision-making in national institutions, on the growing concentration of power in the hands of the prime minister? Part of the answer is that the Canadian Senate is such a clear exception among federal systems across the world; no other democratic federal state has an upper house staffed by federal government appointees — actually prime ministerial appointees — with no input from the governments or citizens of the provinces they are deemed to represent. (Senators are appointed by the prime minister of the day and serve until age 75.) Other federal states use their upper chambers to articulate rather than ignore federal principles, to provide territorial representation that complements and supplements representation by population in the lower house. The Canadian Senate is all but impossible to explain, much less defend, to international or, for that matter, national audiences.

Perhaps a large part of the answer for the concentration of the reform impetus on the Senate is that the Senate is a relatively easy target. Senators lack much in the way of public credibility; they are seen, not without reason, as individuals reaping the financial rewards for service to the governing party of the day they were appointed. No one will come to the defense of the Senate, whereas the House has proven to be a very effective defender of institutional arrangements that often seem out of date. Moreover, as we will see in the conclusion to this section, Senate reform is the best trigger to pull in order to initiate other forms of parliamentary reform.

What, then, are the principles that western Canadians would like to see embedded within a reformed Senate? The following reflect a strong regional consensus:

1. Senators should be elected. Western Canadians display no enthusiasm whatsoever for the present method of Senators appointed by the prime minister and have expressed little more enthusiasm for

Senators appointed by provincial governments. Election is a
consensual value, one very much in step with the democratic spirit
of the times and the democratic face that Canada tries to project to
the international community. There is, however, no consensus on,
and little public discussion of, the specific means by which
Senators might be elected.

2. The Senate should have some autonomous field of action, some
policy leverage that is not subject to override by the House of
Commons.

3. This said, western Canadians would also prefer a parliamentary
order in which the House of Commons was the primary legislative
assembly.

4. The Senate should provide some counterweight to the principle of
representation by population in the House of Commons.

These conditions could be met by the Triple E model that dominates
Senate reform discussions in the West — a Senate based on direct popular election, equality of representation for the provinces, and some
significant measure of legislative influence. However, it is not clear that
strict provincial equality would serve western Canadian interests well.
It would provide tremendous leverage for Atlantic Canada's four
provinces, home to only 7.6 per cent (and falling) of the national population; Atlantic Canada would have a slightly smaller proportion of the
new Senators, but those individuals would yield much more clout than
do their existing counterparts. However, an equal Senate would do less
for Alberta, with 9.9 per cent of the national population, and British
Columbia with 13.0 per cent.[8] There is, then, some room for negotia-
tion with respect to provincial equality, whereas there is no room on the
principle of direct popular election.

Senate reform is important in its own right as it would provide a check
on the power of the prime minister and cabinet, and a counterweight to
representation by population. A reformed Senate would add some badly
needed institutional muscle to the federal nature of Canada. Senate

reform, however, could also trigger other much-needed reforms. A different election format for the Senate might stimulate interest in electoral reform for the House of Commons. A reformed Senate might lead to parliamentary reforms designed to enhance the status of MPs and reduce the weight of party discipline in the House. As William Thorsell argues:

> Whatever the odds of success, the next great Canadian cause should be reform of our electoral and parliamentary systems to require much more negotiation among political persuasions and regions through the life of any parliament. Our zero-sum democracy needs to move to a 60-40 democracy, where majorities prevail only after having to respond to other interests and opinions. The process of politics between elections must be meaningful if the elections are to be meaningful — and if Canada is to be claimed by all its people. Through its direct spending power, meanwhile, the federal government should assume a much higher profile in the lives of ordinary Canadians where they live — in cities and suburbs in every region, even the prosperous ones. Calgary won't mind.[9]

The point to stress is that the higher federal government profile that Thorsell recommends can be brought about only if it is wedded to, in fact preceded by, meaningful institutional reform.

PARADOX OF CONSTITUTIONAL CHANGE

Canada's troubled history with constitutional reform carries two important messages. The first is that western Canadian discontent is not sufficient to ignite or drive constitutional change. Perhaps because that discontent is never linked to a credible separatist threat, it is neither a necessary nor sufficient condition for a national debate on constitutional reform. Witness, for example, the lack of any progress on the Senate reform file. The constitutional reform process is driven by discontent in Quebec, which is a necessary and, when linked to a credible separatism threat, a sufficient condition. However, the second message is that

although Quebec rather than the West drives the process, the *results* do
not necessarily reflect the constitutional aspirations or even interests of
Quebec. The 1982 Constitution Act bears a much closer resemblance to
western Canadian constitutional visions than it does to the constitutional
visions in Quebec, federalist or sovereigntist, that prevailed in the late
1970s and early 1980s. Western Canadians never speak of the "betrayal"
of the 1982 Constitution Act.

At first glance, and indeed at second and third glance, the prospects
for institutional change appear to be bleak. There is apparently little
appetite in the country for constitutional change, and it is difficult to
go very far down the institutional reform path without running up
against the need for constitutional change. However, the prospects may
not be as remote as is often assumed. The institutional reform debate
could break open for a number of reasons:

1. The independence movement could rise again in Quebec. Perhaps
   more likely, the election of a federalist government in Quebec
   could re-open the debate about a renewed federalism.
2. Debates about continental integration could bring institutional
   reform into play.
3. We could confront a democratic crisis in the Senate, perhaps
   where an incoming Canadian Alliance government confronts a
   Senate in which it has no representation. In such a scenario, it
   would be foolish to expect the Liberal-dominated Senate to
   acquiesce to the legislative agenda brought forward by an Alliance
   government. At some point we will see a change of government in
   Ottawa, and at that point the new government will confront a
   Senate in which the Liberal majority will have been entrenched
   for a generation.
4. We may have constitutional change forced upon us by developments with respect to Aboriginal self-government, by the northern
   territories' quest for provincial recognition, by the push from the

cities for constitutional recognition, or by a crisis with the Royal Family in Britain.

5. Continuing regional cleavages within the party system may impede effective government in Canada to the point where the risks of undertaking constitutional change become tolerable.

6. Senate reform may reappear on the agenda of national political parties.

7. Canadians at large, and western Canadians in particular, may grow to be fed up with political institutions that are so badly out of step with our understanding of democracy in the twenty-first century.

It would be foolish, therefore, to dismiss the long term prospects for fundamental constitutional and institutional reform even though at present there appears to be little public appetite. Such reform has been accomplished by other countries, and there is no reason to believe that Canada will remain forever a backwater with respect to the currents of democratic reform found throughout the western world. For example, Australia, Britain, and New Zealand have all achieved, or are contemplating, institutional reforms equal in magnitude to Senate reform in Canada. It is important, therefore, to have an understanding of what might be done should the opportunity arise. History tells us that it is unlikely that the West could create or drive a national institutional reform agenda — the impetus, as always, is more likely to come from Quebec — but western Canadians should be ready when opportunity next presents itself. Although any drive for constitutional change is more likely to focus on democratic reform than on enhancing regional representation — such as reigning in the powers of the prime minister and the Prime Minister's Office and addressing the election of unchecked majority governments by a minority of the electorate — there is no reason why issues of regional representation could not be included in the reform agenda.

A PARLIAMENT FOR WESTERN CANADA?

One of the more creative — and radical — proposals for constitutional change has come from Wayne Eyre, a Saskatoon writer and editor.[10] Eyre has proposed a "loose east-west confederation within the larger Canadian dominion with one Parliament in Ottawa, another in the West." The existing Parliament in Ottawa would continue to exercise jurisdiction over such matters as defence, foreign policy and macro-economic policy, while provincial governments in the West would be folded into the regional parliament, modeled in principle along the lines of the new legislative assemblies in Scotland and Wales. As Eyre suggests, "Western Canada would become analogous to Scotland; Ottawa, to Westminster; Canada, to the U.K." Home rule for the West would facilitate legislation that would "better reflect western sensibilities and priorities." As a consequence, "western alienation would evaporate; easterners would continue on, happy in Ottawa-land."

At the very least, a western Parliament would provide an institutional vehicle for addressing pan-regional issues. However, the abolition of existing provincial governments would certainly be seen by most western Canadians as a step too far.

It is also important that regional discussions of institutional and constitution reform look forward as well as back. While the flaws of existing parliamentary institutions should be addressed, attention must be paid to the effective incorporation of Aboriginal peoples and the northern territories. Perhaps of even greater importance, Canadians must address the constitutional and institutional standing of the metropolitan centres that are increasingly dominating Canadian life.

Urban Sites for Multi-Level Governance

It is difficult to go very far in any discussion of policy interdependence and multi-level governance without running smack into Canadian cities. As noted in previous chapters, Canada is a highly urbanized country, and nowhere is this more true than in the West. Calgary's population, for example, now exceeds that of any of the Atlantic provinces, and the population of metropolitan Vancouver at the time of the 2001 Census was equivalent to 86 per cent of the total Atlantic population. The cities, it should be stressed, carry more than numerical clout. They are widely recognized as the primary drivers of the new, knowledge-based economy, the incubators for human capital, centres for the arts, and magnets for international immigration. The health and vitality of Canada's major metropolitan areas will be a key determinant of our success in global competition. As a consequence, urban affairs can only climb on the nation's political agenda in the years to come, something that has been recognized by the Prime Minister's Caucus Task Force on Urban Affairs and by the prominence of urban affairs within the platforms of federal parties, with the Canadian Alliance being a puzzling exception.

The emerging urban agenda is both large and complex. It embraces financial resources and taxation tools, urban infrastructure, the continued vitality of the arts communities, immigrant absorption, and multiculturalism. At times, it embraces a robust debate on the potential constitutional recognition of cities. In the context of the present discussion, however, the important point to note is that cities already are sites for multi-level governance. The programs of not only municipal governments but also the provincial and federal governments have an immediate impact on the health and international competitiveness of Canadian cities. Municipal governments are necessarily engaged with their provincial and federal counterparts, and the intensity of this engagement will increase. Whether this will necessitate some adjustment in the constitutional and institutional configuration of the Canadian federal state is still open to question.[11] However, what is not open to question is that the cities will provide the primary test in the years ahead for Canada's capacity to handle policy interdependence and multi-level governance.

URBAN ABORIGINAL POLICY

An excellent example of the complexities of multi-level governance and the realities of policy interdependence comes from the set of policies and programs now in place for Aboriginal peoples living in western Canada's major urban centers. Both the federal and provincial governments are active with programs of universal application but of direct relevance for Aboriginal residents, with general programs whose delivery is tailored in part for Aboriginal peoples, and with programs designed explicitly for Aboriginal peoples.[12] Municipal governments are also active with respect to policing, cultural policies, recreational activities, and homeless shelters. School boards may have special programs and facilities, and regional health authorities attempt to respond to the particular dynamics of Aboriginal health. In some cases, neighbouring First Nations governments provide outreach services for their residents living in urban environments. And, as a final complication, many government programs are delivered through Aboriginal and non-Aboriginal not-for-profit organizations. To say that the maze of policies, programs, responsibilities, and funding is complex only begins to capture the labyrinth within which urban Aboriginal Canadians function. At the same time, to argue that only one government should handle this difficult file is to ignore the realities of policy interdependence. All governments *are* involved whether they like it or not.

The emergence of an urban agenda poses some significant challenges for western Canada. It cannot be assured, for example, that a national urban strategy articulated through the existing political parties and parliamentary institutions will give full weight to the urban character of western Canada. There is a risk it may boil down to a Montreal/Toronto strategy, one that equates the renewal of the Toronto waterfront and the economic competitiveness of Montreal as synonymous with the national interest. An urban agenda could also become entangled with the east/west divide within the West, with most of the urban growth occurring in Alberta and British Columbia. Finally, and by no means least, the urban agenda brings into bold relief the more precarious demographic, economic, and social status of the rural West.

As George Melnyk explains, cities were seen as a blight on traditional images of the West:

> The attempt to exclude urban life from the image of the West is rooted in a deep anti-urban bias that runs through our heritage and has its roots as far back as Roman times, when the city was portrayed as a source of intrigue, decadence and indulgence, while the countryside was heralded as the home of virtue. Christian religious fundamentalism enhanced this attitude by denouncing cities as the sources of sin, where temptation and vice lurked for the unwary innocents from the countryside. This bias imprinted itself on the prairie mind. Not only were prairie cities full of dangers, but they were also derivative, nothing more than the re-creations of nineteenth-century Eastern Canadian cities. There was nothing original here, just a carbon copy of what was already established elsewhere. The soul of the West was in the countryside.[13]

While this may not be an easy orientation to shake, shake it we must, for as Melnyk concludes, "the city is the technological hub of cyberspace, the new geography of the twenty-first century, and it is this geography that is transforming who and what we are."[14] It is more than time for the "soul of the West" to move to the urban heartland.

Strategic Partnerships

The case for the end of governments operating in splendid isolation applies with equal force to the region as a whole. The West is not an island unto itself within Canada or within the continental and global economies. Therefore, just as interprovincial partnerships within the West are likely to become more important in the future, so too are strategic partnerships with communities and interests outside the region.[15] Here a number of possibilities come to mind.

Potential energy developments in the northern territories, including a Mackenzie Valley pipeline, pipeline connections to Alaskan natural gas fields, and energy plays in the Arctic Ocean, could all have a substantial economic impact on the prosperity of the western provinces. In fact, the potential southern impact may even exceed that on the northern territories themselves. A great deal of the engineering work, transportation activity, purchase of materials and equipment, and labour pool will come from the provinces, and a great deal of the financial benefits will stick to the south. For example, Edmonton's role as the gateway to the North affords the city, and indirectly the province, tremendous opportunities. There is, then, a complementarity between the economic interests of the North and West, and managing this complementarity is an important political task.

THE ALBERTA-QUEBEC CONSTITUTIONAL PARTNERSHIP

Although not generally recognized, even by their respective electorates, the Alberta and Quebec governments, including sovereigntist governments in Quebec, have often been constitutional allies in the past. The two governments have shared common concerns about federal intrusions into provincial fields of jurisdiction, about the broad application of the federal spending power, and, more generally, about respect for the federal principles of the Canadian constitution. In tussles with the federal government and at times with other provincial governments, Quebec has given Alberta the political muscle it would otherwise lack, while Alberta has helped universalize Quebec's constitutional position beyond the rhetoric of sovereignty or sovereignty-association. However, the two governments have not agreed across the board. The constitutional recognition of Quebec as a distinct society has been and remains a flash point in Alberta, and Quebec and Alberta have not agreed on the necessity of reforming parliamentary institutions. Alberta has championed Senate reform, seeking greater regional leverage on national policy, whereas Quebec has had little complaint with regards to its existing leverage in Ottawa. Canada's brief nine-month experience with an Alberta prime minister, Joe Clark, pales beyond significance when compared to the successive federal regimes of Pierre Trudeau, Brian Mulroney, and Jean Chrétien, all Quebecers. (If we throw British Columbia's John Turner and Kim Campbell into the post-1960s mix, not a whole lot changes.) More fundamentally, Alberta and Quebec have never aligned on a separatist agenda. As Edward Greenspoon wrote in a column about the lack of support for the Alberta Independence Party, "No Westerner would ever mock the flag; their complaint is that the politicians are disgracing it."[16] To the extent that Quebec continues to pursue a policy of disengagement from the intergovernmental mainstream, as evidenced by its decision not to endorse the Social Union Framework Agreement, Alberta's intergovernmental weight will be reduced.

Energy developments off the coasts of Newfoundland and Nova Scotia also open up new possibilities for strategic regional partnerships. There is a shared interest in protecting provincial jurisdiction over, and ownership of, natural resources, and a shared interest in national policies designed to foster rather than impair a robust Canadian energy sector. Potential oil and natural gas deposits near the Queen Charlotte Islands in British Columbia increase the geographical scope of shared interests. Although opportunities for regional alliances have seldom been explored in the past, they may become more important in the future. It should be noted, however, that the West's historical relationship with Atlantic Canada has been far from smooth. The residents of Nova Scotia and New Brunswick in particular often saw western Canadian growth as coming at the expense of their own region, and western Canadian perspectives on the national community often stopped at "Central Canada." Just as western Canadians have complained that "national" visions too frequently ignore the West, national visions emerging from the West too often pay only glancing attention to Atlantic Canada. If effective strategic partnerships are to evolve, broader national visions may be needed on both sides of the continent. (They may also be needed in Quebec and Ontario, but that is another story.)

Even the potential of strategic partnerships with Ontario should not be dismissed out of hand. Over the past decade, for example, Conservative governments in Alberta and Ontario have often seen eye to eye on matters of public policy, and their perspectives on federalism have often aligned. The debate over the ratification of the Kyoto Accord demonstrated that intergovernmental alliances do not always follow conventional regional lines. The historical assumption that the West and Ontario are necessarily at loggerheads no longer fits the complex policy realities and debates in contemporary Canada.

State governments in the American northwest open up another venue for strategic partnerships. There has been a long history of bilateral relationships between state and provincial governments in the western part of the continent. While in the past those relationships tended to be informal, irregular, and at a modest level in the political hierarchy, there are signs today that they are becoming more regular.[17] Broader forums for interaction include the Pacific North-West Economic Region (PNWER) that incorporates Alaska, Alberta, British Columbia, Idaho, Montana, Oregon, Washington, and the Yukon, and which provides a low profile forum for the discussion of both economic issues common to the region and regional collaboration. There has also been considerable if more abstract discussion of Cascadia, a bio-region along the western side of the coastal range that includes at the very least the shared watershed environments of British Columbia and Washington and at times is extended conceptually from northern California to Alaska.[18] These tentative steps have not bridged the deep Canadian-American divide over softwood lumber, but they do provide an initial forum within which to explore regional partnerships across state, provincial, and international borders. Although such partnerships are unlikely to approach the economic importance of regional partnerships in the European Union, they should not be ignored. With the growing volume of north-south trade and the relative decline of east-west trade, regional organizations spanning the international border are bound to take on more weight.

We should also note the need for strategic partnerships with the First Nations communities found across the West. Resource and human capital development, tourism, and environmental protection hinge on achieving an effective intergovernmental relationship within which common interests can be pursued and conflicts addressed. This may take some time and will undoubtedly be conditional on the settlement of land claims and the full institutionalization of First Nations governments. Still, it is a distant goal towards which we can begin to move, indeed must begin to move as a regional community.

Finally, it should be stressed that intergovernmental partnerships and alliances, while important, are by no means the full story. Transboundary Canadian-American associations and partnerships abound in virtually every aspect of the society and economy — professional organizations, sports leagues including the National Hockey League, fraternal associations such as the Lions and the Rotary clubs, and business and labour associations. Although to date these are rarely organized on a regional basis, this may happen with greater frequency as economic ties between the western provinces and states expand and deepen.

Conclusions

The emerging governance landscape in western Canada is built around a number of prominent features: greater inter-provincial collaboration, strategic alliances, more salient urban governments, and, hopefully, a more cooperative style of federal-provincial relations. Above all else, this landscape is characterized by multi-level governance and policy interdependence. If western Canadians and their governments can function effectively within this landscape, they may well be able to leave a positive mark on the Canadian whole. However, if this new governance landscape is to provide an adequate foundation for regional prosperity, a number of changes will have to occur. At the very least, we will need:

- a more effective policy and political voice for the major cities in western Canada;
- a more effective Aboriginal voice within the networks of inter-governmental relations; and
- federal parliamentary institutions better able to reflect and express regional interests and aspirations.

If we cannot move on these fronts, then it will be more difficult to meet regional challenges and realize regional opportunities.

Canadians often take pride, perhaps unwarranted pride, in offering a model for the world of a reasonably harmonious multicultural and bilingual community able to provide its citizens with a high level of prosperity and security. This assessment, however, is not universally shared either outside the country (where people are more likely to ignore rather than contest the Canadian vision) or within. Aboriginal peoples have certainly expressed serious reservations, as have nationalists and even federalists within Quebec. And, as this book has shown, western Canadians have long expressed a more guarded view of the Canadian political system. If we are indeed to provide a model for the rest of the world, we need to do a better job at managing our own political affairs. We need to demonstrate an ability to handle both regional conflict and urban realities in order to demonstrate that we have political institutions well-equipped for the contemporary challenges from an interdependent world. Here we have some considerable distance to go.

Notes

[1] David G. Wood, *The Lougheed Legacy* (Toronto, ON: Key Porter Books,1985) 242-43.

[2] The tax competitiveness of the western Canadian provinces is a policy area fraught with mythologies, incomplete data, and rapidly changing tax rates. For example, although Saskatchewan is commonly seen as a high-tax regime compared to neighbouring Alberta, Saskatchewan's Minister of Industry and Resources, Eldon Lautermilch, points out that the average Saskatchewan family in 2002 paid only $92 more in taxes and utility fees than its Alberta counterpart, a spread that has shrunk from $1,961 in 1993. Michelle Harris, "The road to success often leads to Alberta," *Macleans* (15 July 2002): 24.

[3] Minutes of the PCWC Steering Committee, March 20, 2002.

[4] Robin Summerfield, "Research will get processing punch: WestGrid shared by BC, Alberta," *Calgary Herald* 18 March 2002: B3.

5   See David Elton, ed., *One Prairie Province?* (Lethbridge, AB: Lethbridge Herald, 1970).

6   Dolphin A3.

7   Carol Harrington, "Trudeau and Western Canada," *The Canadian Press* 29 September 2000.

8   Equality of representation would make no sense for the northern territories. Nonetheless, these rapidly evolving political communities would have to be incorporated in a reformed Senate.

9   William Thorsell, "It's time to tackle the next great Canadian cause," *The Globe and Mail* 25 March 2002: A15.

10   Wayne Eyre, "A bonnie West awaits," *The Vancouver Sun* 16 May 2001: A15.

11   For a detailed discussion of this point, see Denis Wong, *Toward Urban Renaissance: Addressing Intergovernmental Structures for Western Canada's Cities* (Calgary, AB: Canada West Foundation, 2002).

12   Calvin Hanselmann, *Urban Aboriginal People in Western Canada: Realities and Policies* (Calgary, AB: Canada West Foundation, 2001); Calvin Hanselmann, *Enhanced Urban Aboriginal Programming in Western Canada* (Calgary, AB: Canada West Foundation, 2002).

13   George Melnyk, *New Moon at Batoche: Reflections on the Urban Prairie* (Banff, AB: The Banff Centre Press, 1999) 89.

14   Melnyk 101.

15   We would like to thank Peter Lougheed and Preston Manning for directing our thoughts in this direction.

16   Edward Greenspoon, "The bottom line: The West wants in, not out," *Globe and Mail* 25 January 2001.

17   Howard Leeson, "Alberta/Saskatchewan Transborder Contacts with US States: A Survey and Analysis Revisited," paper presented at the Conference on Managing Tensions: Evaluating the Institutions of the Federation, Kingston, ON, 2-3 November 2001.

18   Elizabeth Nickson, "The Last Best Place," *National Post* 7 July 2001: B3. Sometimes Cascadia is extended even further to include Alberta, Idaho, and Montana. See Brent Jang, "'New West' inches south of the border," *Globe and Mail* 13 May 2002: B9.

MOVING FORWARD

"What has been sought and to some degree achieved [in Canada] is not really unification or consolidation, but the articulation of regional patterns in one transcontinental state."[1]

—J.M.S. CARELESS, historian

Western Canada is a region marked by great promise and great aspirations. As *Western Visions, Western Futures* has shown, the West has considerable assets — an energetic and diverse population, myriad natural resources, a strong economy, and a long history of multiculturalism, hard work and innovation. In many ways, however, it is precisely this promise that gives rise to continued feelings of western alienation: western Canadians are concerned and quite often convinced that their aspirations are not shared by the rest of Canada, and worse, that conflicting "national" goals will work to undermine the interests of the West.

Thus, what Canadians need to understand — and, indeed, what is often so difficult for people and politicians outside the West to understand — is that western Canadian aspirations and alienation are two sides of the same coin. It is *because* of regional optimism that western Canadians often feel so alienated from the rest of Canada or, more specifically, from the federal government. The perception, based on recent and not-so-recent history, is that the rules of the game in national politics are tipped against the West and that the rest of the country does not value the West's contribution to the national community. The perception is that, when push comes to shove (or even sooner), Canadians through their national government will easily adopt policies that damage or undermine the West if these policies are felt to benefit other regions. Western alienation, therefore, is not a whine about the past, but rather a heart-felt concern about the future — based on the assumption that the best predictor of future behaviour on the part of the national government is past behaviour.

This then begs the question: how can regional aspirations be met and what is the role of the rest of Canada — and, in particular, the federal government — in realizing these aspirations? *Western Visions, Western Futures* outlines a number of process and policy options for federal and provincial governments alike. But the first step must be a recognition, by elected officials, business leaders and the general public, that the West is a critically important region to Canada, and that leaving western alienation unaddressed for another five or 50 years will only serve to weaken or perhaps destroy Canada.

This reality grows ever more apparent in the current international context. Globalization increasingly means that geographic identities and affiliations are fluid — a change that threatens the importance of nations and national communities. A country that fails to successfully deal with regional discontent is not doing itself any favours. As noted in Chapter 1, Canada's failure to tackle regional discontent with energy and resolve places the country under continual strain. In the interests of national unity *and prosperity*, Canada must take western alienation seriously.

It is hoped that *Western Visions, Western Futures* will help Canadians understand the dynamics of western Canada and more fully appreciate the importance of the West to the broader national community. The future prosperity and well-being of Canada are integrally tied to the future of the West. For this reason, western visions must be part of our national visions, and the western future understood as part of our national future. As noted earlier, historian J.M.S Careless suggests a vision that allows "the articulation of regional patterns in one transcontinental state." Such a holistic national approach — one that fully incorporates the West — will benefit all of Canada.

Note

[1] J.M.S. Careless, "'Limited Identities' in Canada," *Canadian Historical Review* 50 (1969): 9.

REFERENCES

Allen, Richard, Ed. *A Region of the Mind*. Regina, SK: Canadian Plains Study Centre, 1973.

Angus Reid Group. "Appendices." *Portrait of a Troubled Country: Canadians and the National Unity Debate*. Canada: Angus Reid Group, 1991.

Archer, J.A. "The Prairie Perspective." *One Country or Two?* Ed. R.M. Burns. Montreal, QC: McGill-Queen's University Press, 1971.

Atlantic Canada Opportunities Agency. www.acoa.ca.

Berdahl, Loleen. *Looking West: A Survey of Western Canadians*. Calgary, AB: Canada West Foundation, 2001.

Berdahl, Loleen, and Sophie Sapergia. *Urban Nation, Federal State*. Calgary, AB: Canada West Foundation, 2001.

Blais, André, Elisabeth Gidengil, Richard Nadeau, and Neil Nevitte. *Anatomy of a Liberal Victory: Making Sense of the Vote in the 2000 Canadian Election*. Peterborough, ON: Broadview Press, 2002.

Bruce, Jean. *The Last Best West*. Toronto, ON: Fitzhenry and Whiteside, 1976.

Burnet, Jean. *Next Year Country: A Study of Rural Social Organization in Alberta*. Toronto, ON: University of Toronto Press, 1978.

Burns, Pat. Editorial. CJOR Radio Vancouver. 10 November 1986. Cited in *The Western Separatist Papers* 11, 9 (September 1993): 3.

Cairns, Alan C. "The Electoral System and the Party System in Canada, 1921–1965." *Canadian Journal of Political Science* 1, 1 (March 1968): 55–80.

Calgary Herald, 27 January 2001, A4.

Campbell, Robert M., and Leslie A. Pal. *The Real World of Canadian Politics: Cases in Process and Policy*. Peterborough, ON: Broadview Press, 1989.

Canada West Foundation. *Public Opinion Update, Report No. 4, June 1980*. Calgary, AB: Canada West Foundation, 1980.

———. *Public Opinion Update, Report No. 7, November 1980*. Calgary, AB: Canada West Foundation, 1980.

———. *Public Opinion Update, Report No. 12, April 1982*. Calgary, AB: Canada West Foundation, 1982.

———. *Public Opinion Update, Report No. 17, December 1983*. Calgary, AB: Canada West Foundation, 1983.

———. *Public Opinion Update, Report No. 18, December 1984*. Calgary, AB: Canada West Foundation, 1984.

Careless, J.M.S. "'Limited Identities' in Canada." *Canadian Historical Review* 50 (1969).

Centre for Research and Information on Canada. *Portraits of Canada 2001*. Montreal, QC: CRIC, 2002.

Creighton, Donald. *The Passionate Observer: Selected Writings*. Toronto, ON: McClelland and Stewart, 1980.

Dolphin, Ric. "Welcome to tales from 'Buffalo Trail.'" *Calgary Herald* 8 May 2002: A3.

Edmonton Sun 28 October 2002: A1.

Elton, David K. "Electoral Perceptions of Federalism: A Descriptive Analysis of the Alberta Electorate." Diss., University of Alberta, 1973.

Elton, David, Ed. *One Prairie Province?* Lethbridge, AB: *Lethbridge Herald*, 1970.

Eyre, Wayne. "A bonnie West awaits." *The Vancouver Sun* 16 May 2001: A15.

Fowke, Vernon C. *Canadian Agricultural Policy: The Historical Pattern*. Toronto, ON: University of Toronto Press, 1947.

———. *The National Policy and the Wheat Economy*. Toronto, ON: University of Toronto Press, 1957.

Friesen, Gerald. *The West: Regional Ambitions, National Debates, Global Age*. Toronto, ON: Penguin, 1999.

Gibbins, Roger. *Building the New West: A Framework for Regional Prosperity*. Calgary, AB: Canada West Foundation, 2001.

————. "Models of Nationalism: A Case Study of Political Ideologies in the Canadian West." *Canadian Journal of Political Science*, 10:2 (June 1977): 341–73.

————. *Prairie Politics and Society: Regionalism in Decline.* Scarborough, ON: Butterworths, 1980.

Gilsdorf, Robert R. "Western Alienation, Political Alienation, and the Federal System: Subjective Perceptions." *Society and Politics in Alberta: Research Papers.* Ed. Carlo Caldarola. Toronto, ON: Methuen, 1979.

Goldfarb, Martin. *The Searching Nation: A Study of Canadians' Attitudes to the Future of Confederation.* Toronto, ON: Southam Press, 1977.

Government of Singapore (n.d.). Baby Bonus Scheme System. http://www.babybonus.gov.sg

Greenspoon, Edward. "The bottom line: The West wants in, not out." *Globe and Mail* 25 January 2001.

Hanselmann, Calvin. *Enhanced Urban Aboriginal Programming in Western Canada.* Calgary, AB: Canada West Foundation, 2002.

————. *Urban Aboriginal People in Western Canada: Realities and Policies.* Calgary, AB: Canada West Foundation, 2001.

Harmsworth, Katherine. *Glocalism: The Growing Importance of Local Space in the Global Environment.* Calgary, AB: Canada West Foundation, December 2001.

Harper, Stephen. "Separation, Alberta-style." *National Post* 8 December 2000: A18.

Harrington, Carol. "Trudeau and Western Canada." *The Canadian Press* 29 September 29, 2000.

Harris, Michelle. "The road to success often leads to Alberta." *Macleans* (15 July 2002): 24.

Howe, Paul, and David Northrup. "Strengthening Canadian Democracy: The Views of Canadians." *Policy Matters* 1,5. (July 2000). Montreal, QC: Institute for Research on Public Policy, 2000.

Jang, Brent. "'New West' inches south of the border." *Globe and Mail* 13 May 2002: B9.

Law Commission of Canada. *Renewing Democracy: Debating Electoral Reform in Canada.* Ottawa, ON: Law Commission of Canada, 2002.

Laycock, David. *Populism and Democratic Thought in the Canadian Prairies, 1910–1945.* Toronto, ON: University of Toronto Press, 1990.

————. "Reforming Canadian Democracy? Institutions and Ideology in the Reform Party Project." *Canadian Journal of Political Science* 27 (June 1994).

Leeson, Howard. "Alberta/Saskatchewan Transborder Contacts with US States: A Survey and Analysis Revisited." Paper presented at the Conference on Managing Tensions: Evaluating the Institutions of the Federation, Kingston, ON, 2–3 November 2001.

Lower, A.R.M. *From Colony to Nation: A History of Canada.* Toronto, ON: Longmans, Green and Company, 1946.

Lunman, Kim. "Canada losing to US in baby race." *Globe and Mail* 4 July 2002: A9.

Mallory, J.R. *Social Credit and the Federal Power in Canada.* Toronto, ON: University of Toronto Press, 1953.

Manitoba Bureau of Statistics. *Manitoba's Aboriginal Populations Projected 1991–2016.* Native Affairs Secretariat, Manitoba Northern Affairs, 1997.

Manning, Preston. *The New Canada.* Toronto, ON: Macmillan, 1992.

Martin, Don. "Your tax dollars at work." *Calgary Herald* 7 May 2002: A3.

May, Howard. "New group to push for Alberta autonomy." *Calgary Herald* 27 January 2001: A4.

McCormick, Peter, Ernest C. Manning, and Gordon Gibson. *Regional Representation: The Canadian Partnership.* Calgary, AB: Canada West Foundation, 1981.

Melnyk, George. *New Moon at Batoche: Reflections on the Urban Prairie.* Banff, AB: The Banff Centre Press, 1999.

Menzies, Peter. "Deregulation process needs stabilization." *Calgary Herald* 29 January 2001: A10.

Mercer, Ilana. "Raise a toast to Western separatism and Canada's good health." *Globe and Mail* 3 January 2001: A11.

Morton, W.L. "The Bias of Prairie Politics." *Transactions of the Royal Society of Canada*, Series III, 49 (June 1955): Section II, 66.

————. *The Progressive Party in Canada.* Toronto, ON: University of Toronto Press, 1950.

National Post 8 March 2002: A14.

Nickson, Elizabeth. "The Last Best Place." *National Post* 7 July 2001: B3.

Norris, Mary Jane, Don Kerr, and Francois Nault. "Projections of the

Population with Aboriginal Identity in Canada, 1991–2016." Royal Commission on Aboriginal Peoples, 1995.

Ovenden, Norm. "West feels left out of Canada." *Calgary Herald* 19 December 2000: A1.

Prairie Child Welfare Consortium (PCWC). Steering Committee. 20 March 2002.

Pratt, Larry, and Garth Stevenson, Eds. *Western Separatism: The Myths, Realities and Dangers.* Edmonton, AB: Hurtig Publishers, 1981.

Richler, Mordecai. "Stop complaining about the brain drain: Jesse Helms may clue into Canada's cultural imperialism." *National Post* 21 August 1999.

Roach, Robert. *Beyond Our Borders: Western Canadian Exports in the Global Market.* Calgary, AB: Canada West Foundation, May 2002.

Roach, Robert, and Loleen Berdahl. *State of the West: Western Canadian Demographic and Economic Trends.* Calgary, AB: Canada West Foundation, 2001.

Saskatoon StarPhoenix, 8 March 2002, A11.

Sharpe, Sydney, and Don Braid. *Storming Babylon: Preston Manning and the Rise of the Reform Party.* Toronto, ON: Key Porter Books, 1992.

Smiley, Donald V. *Canada in Question: Federalism in the Seventies.* 2nd ed. Toronto, ON: McGraw-Hill, 1976.

Smith, David E. "Party Government, Representation and National Integration in Canada." *Party Government and Regional Representation in Canada.* Ed. Peter Aucoin. Toronto, ON: University of Toronto Press, 1985.

———. *Prairie Liberalism: The Liberal Party in Saskatchewan, 1905–1971.* Toronto, ON: University of Toronto Press, 1975.

———. "The Prairie Provinces." *The Provincial Political Systems: Comparative Essays.* Ed. David J. Bellamy, Jon H. Pammett, and Donald C. Rowat. Toronto, ON: Methuen, 1976.

———. "Western Politics and National Unity." *Canada and the Burden of Unity.* Ed. David Jay Bercuson. Toronto, ON: Macmillan, 1977.

Smith, Denis. "Liberals and Conservatives on the Prairies, 1917–1968." *Prairie Perspectives.* Ed. David P. Gagan. Toronto, ON: Holt, Rinehart and Winston, 1970.

Summerfield, Robin. "Research will get processing punch: WestGrid shared by BC, Alberta." *Calgary Herald* 18 March 2002: B3.

Thorsell, William. "It's time to tackle the next great Canadian cause." *The Globe and Mail* 25 March 2002: A15.

Underhill, Frank H. *In Search of Canadian Liberalism*. Toronto, ON: Macmillan, 1960.

Wente, Margaret, Ed., *I Never Say Anything Provocative*. Toronto, ON: Peter Martin, 1975.

"Western Alienation: A *This Morning* Roundtable." *Policy Options* (April 2001): 7.

Western Economic Diversification, <www.wd.gc.ca>.

"What the West wants." *Calgary Herald* 27 January 2001: OS6.

Wong, Denis. *Toward Urban Renaissance: Addressing Intergovernmental Structures for Western Canada's Cities*. Calgary, AB: Canada West Foundation, 2002.

Wood, David G. *The Lougheed Legacy*. Toronto, ON: Key Porter Books, 1985.

Yaffe, Barbara. "Ottawa finds yet another way to ruin Canadian businesses." *Calgary Herald* 6 March 2002: A13.

———. "Separation a recipe for stagnation." *Calgary Herald* 8 January 2001: A10.

INDEX

Ablonczy, Diane, 24, 60
Aboriginal people, 3, 7, 17, 106, 198, 205–6
   Aboriginal/non-Aboriginal relations,
      18, 149–50, 186
   age of, 8
   engagement in labour force, 153–54,
      172
   federal government responsibility for,
      8, 200
   labour pool, 18
   legacy of colonialism, 170
   multi-level governance, 179, 200
   policy issues, 170–71
   population growth, 148
   prosperity, 150
   self government, 168, 178, 191, 196
   significance to western Canada, 148–49
   urban, 150, 170, 200
ACOA. *See* Atlantic Canada Opportunities
   Agency (ACOA)
Action Démocratique du Quebec (ADQ),
   108
age, 3, 142–46, 149
   Aboriginal population, 8
   as factor in western alienation, 80, 108–9
agrarian West, 66
   populist parties, 44, 82
Agreement on Internal Trade, 154
agricultural bio-tech industry (proposed),
   161
agricultural subsidies, 98
   American, 159
airline competition, 93
airport security tax, 105

Alaska, 204
Alberta, 82–84
   alienation, 4, 59, 68–71, 74, 77
   as Conservative stronghold, 45
   debt reduction, 164–65
   deficit issues, 162
   equity and fairness, 102
   firewall strategy, 121–23
   formation, 7
   GDP growth, 156
   immigration "bounce," 146
   international exports, 157–58
   interprovincial migration, 138
   oil and natural gas, 160
   population, 134–35
   regional identification, 13–14
   Senate reform and, 194
   seniors, 142
   separatism, 127–28
   strategic partnerships, 204
   under-representation, 55–56, 115–16
   urbanization, 151
"The Alberta Advantage," 179
Alberta Independence Party, 126, 203
Alberta Pension Plan (proposed), 121
Alberta-Quebec constitutional partnership,
   202–3
Alberta Union of Municipal Associations,
   166
alienation. *See* western alienation
American markets. *See* Canadian-American
   trade
American protectionism, 157
   agricultural subsidies, 159